# THE
# CAT
# GURU

## NAINA LEPES

IBIS PRESS
*Berwick, Maine*

First published in 2004 by
IBIS PRESS
an imprint of Nicolas-Hays, Inc.
P. O. Box 1126
Berwick, ME 03901-1126
Distributed to the trade by
Red Wheel/Weiser, LLC
P. O. Box 612
York Beach, ME 03910-0612
www.redwheelweiser.com

**Library of Congress Cataloging-in-Publication Data**
Lepes, Naina.
The cat guru / Naina Lepes.-- 1st American pbk. ed.
p. cm.
ISBN 0-89254-099-0 (pbk. : alk. paper)
1. Lepes, Naina. 2. Religious life--Hinduism. I. Title.
BL1237.32.L47 2004
294.5'4--dc22                                          2004013807

VG
Cover and text design by Kathryn Sky-Peck.
Typeset in Minion
Printed in the United States of America

10  09  08  07  06  05  04
7  6  5  4  3  2  1

The paper used in this publication meets the minimum requirements of the
American National Standard for Information Sciences—Permanence of Paper for
Printed Library Materials Z39.48–1992 (R1997).

This book is dedicated to

Sweetie, Bhakti, Samah, Tom, the two Lucifer Juniors,

Neffy, Merlyn, Gershwin, Henrietta, Delphi, and

all cats both wild and pedigree

who are here to show us

the art of

love without attachment

duty combined with freedom

acceptance filled with joy and

the total spontaneity that comes from

living in the moment in harmony

with our all-knowing nature.

# CONTENTS

# PLATES

# ACKNOWLEDGMENTS

WITH HEARTFELT GRATITUDE TO:
Jack Donaghy for help scanning the pictures;
Krishna Ghosh for help with the Sanskrit;
Ashish Pathak for responding to my cat questions;
the friends and well-wishers who read the
manuscript and offered their feedback:
Andrea, Ann, Bobby, Cassia, Cathy, Lilly, Meg, Michele, Mimi, Pat,
Retno, Smriti, Sudha and Wendy;
and everyone else who contributed to bringing this book to fruition,
whether up front or behind the scenes.

# PREFACE

WHEN I OFFERED A BEAUTIFUL SEMIWILD cat the opportunity to
have her next litter in my room at an ashram in India, it never dawned on
me that I would be writing about it. But as events began to unfold, the life
of this cat family was filled with so much wonder, and these beautiful
felines touched my own psyche so deeply that I wanted to share the experience with others.

Interwoven throughout the telling, the levels of story expanded from
a simple tale chock full of surprises, humor, love, and pathos to an inner
psychological process, which included my reactions to the events—
whether known or surmised. Both these levels are supported by the spiritual insights that were continually being offered, as the cats became my
teachers.

Though the story might bring out different subjective responses in
each reader, it is my wish that the spiritual teachings that emerged be universal, yet applied in an individual way. Footnotes and glossary are added
for those who might be interested in Indian philosophy and spirituality.

Welcome to the realm of the cat guru!

# 1

## THE SURPRISE

*And the gods descended from heaven*
*in the form of the animal*
*to perform a great sacrifice*
*for humankind*

It is difficult to say when the story really began. But for me, it started on a sultry July morning in south India at Sai Baba's ashram in Puttaparthi. I walked up four flights of stairs and was about to turn the corner on the veranda toward my room when I thought I heard a little squeak. It seemed to be coming from the mattress on the floor. Silently, I peeked between the folds, and what did I find? It was Sweetie, a black-and-white, fat cat. And she was feeding three newborn kittens who looked more like mice than kittens.

I couldn't see them very well because they were so tiny and Sweetie was quite large and covered them all. But what I remember of my first impression was skinny curly tails, full-grown fur, and an all-pervading sense of joy and wonder.

They couldn't have been more than a day old. Maybe they were there when I left in the morning and I just didn't see them. This was the first time I'd ever seen infant kittens, and they made me feel very happy. Yet at the same time I didn't want to intrude. Did Sweetie mind my human presence? She was fully absorbed in her duty of nursing and barely seemed to notice me. I went to get some milk. She lapped it up with hearty abandon.

Whenever I passed the mattress I would just stop and look. I didn't want to touch the kittens, because I remembered what happened to baby birds who were handled by humans. So I just watched. But it was very difficult to remain quiet. For these baby kittens had personalities already from birth. Nature had given them the mechanisms needed to survive. Not only was their theme song "go for the breast," but also "prevent the other guy from getting to the breast."

Two of them were gray-and-white striped liked the father, and one was black and white like the mother. The striped ones, whom I assumed to be male, seemed to be ganging up on the black-and-white one to keep her away from the breast. This upset me terribly. After all, Sweetie had many nipples—certainly enough to go around. And yet, the two boys were willfully keeping the girl away from her survival food. Even if the mother noticed what was happening, she played dumb. This Great Mother was simply there for whoever would come and take what she had to give. She was so one-pointed in her *dharma*[1] of giving that she didn't concern herself with issues of survival or fairness. She only gave what she had come to give and allowed nature to take its course without any mental guidance on her part.

But I was different. I hadn't yet reached Sweetie's level of detachment and acceptance. I felt obliged to work for "justice." And this created a terrible conflict. On the one hand, I didn't want to touch the baby kittens because I thought Sweetie wouldn't like it and might abandon them. On the other hand, I felt I had to intervene to protect the girl from starving. So what ended up happening? I started talking to the striped baby boys and told them to stop pushing their sister away from the breast. When

---

1 *Dharma* means duty, righteousness, the essence of a thing. It stems from the root *dhr*, to support. According to an Indian proverb, "Dharma supports those who support dharma."

they ignored my words, I found myself getting more and more aggravated. Soon I began to wonder what was really going on.

Could these kittens be the catalyst for teaching me the true laws of nature? Was my "justice" any better than nature's "justice"? Could their living presence demonstrate the spot where mind superimposes itself on nature's law? And could they be helping me once and for all to cleanse away all archaic vestiges of inner sibling rivalry?

So alongside the wonder and the love and the gratitude for the privilege of witnessing nature's miracles, there also lurked the underlying suspicion that I was being called upon to learn. And the cat was my guru.

# 2

## THE EXIT

After about a week, Sweetie and the kittens disappeared. I began to feel a bit anxious. There were people in the building who didn't like cats. One person was complaining because Sweetie had diarrhea. And the maid would hit her with the broom whenever she thought no one was looking. Although I was living in the ashram Prashanti Nilayam, which means, "abode of peace," some of the people here were definitely not nonviolent. Could any of them possibly harm the kittens? I let go of this unthinkable thought while my reason accepted that Sweetie had just decided to move them. Only later would I come to know why.

I went about my daily life, while making a few inquiries, and a few days later the boys next door said they had seen Sweetie and the babies outside sitting in the sun. Soon they appeared again on the fifth floor landing, living amidst dust and paint, broken glass, rusty nails, and smelly cleaning oil. This was a junkyard for the workmen. What a spot Sweetie had chosen for rearing her babies—inside a filthy wooden window frame where the three of them rested peacefully, as if they were sleeping in a comfortable nursery. They were about a foot from the fifth-story drop, which remained unprotected.

No fence, no gate. Just a sheer drop down five flights of stairs! The babies could easily fall.

The least I could do was clean up the mess, erect a cardboard gate, and try to make Sweetie's new home more hospitable. It might not have mattered much to them, but it did to me. That evening I worked really hard.

Early the next morning I brought up some milk. The mom had gone hunting and left the babies alone. Something about this spot made me feel very uneasy. I really didn't like it. Sweetie must have chosen it because it was warm and out of the way of hostile humans with their dreaded brooms and glaring ill will. I wished she would bring the kittens into my room. She did not.

The next day it happened. Loud screeches and catcalls. Maybe the father was fighting. I thought it was coming from the street. Only later when I returned to visit the kittens did I see what had really happened. The kittens were barely recognizable. The sight was unbearably gory. The little black-and-white one had been gouged in the belly, and her guts were spilling out. The little gray ones had been bitten on the neck, leaving blood caked around the jugular.

Sweetie just sat there, no longer in the same window frame with the dead kittens. She didn't seem agitated. She didn't seem upset. Did she know what had happened?

I don't think she could conceive of the murder of her babies. Even though she had been present, even though her dead kittens were lying there, even though she must have fought the father tooth and nail to keep them alive, she seemed to have blocked it out totally.

I was utterly devastated. How could this happen? Was the culprit the father? If the killer had been another animal, wouldn't it have eaten the kittens?

I remembered seeing a TV show about wild barnyard cats. It had informed an unsuspecting public that some fathers try to kill their kittens. At the time, I found it hard to believe. Never could I have imagined that this brutal drama would play out so close to home. How could Tom be such a brute as to kill his own beautiful defenseless infants? Was this an aberration or was it normal cat behavior? What would motivate such cold, cruel violence?

As a witness to the slaughter of the innocents, I cringed with disgust. Violent death at any age is horrible, but at two and a half weeks old it seemed unbearable. All the stories I knew about reincarnation and liberation did not help me now. I knew that only the body dies, that at some level there is no such thing as death. And still I was disgusted. Still I was devastated. As I buried the babies and sprinkled their bloody bodies with holy ash, the tears flowed uncontrollably. I was very, very sad. And I was really angry at God. The next day, an unsuspecting acquaintance remarked, "You look gray."

# 3

## IMPECCABLE COMPREHENSION

I had always viewed Mother Nature as basically benevolent. Though I knew of the fury of earthquakes and floods and had experienced two hurricanes as a child, these remained impersonal, abstract, a segmented part of my psyche. Intellectually, I saw the devastating aspects of nature as serving some cosmic purpose—restoring equilibrium and harmony to an ever-evolving universe. But what higher purpose could possibly be served by a father killing his own babies? Why would nature program into him the sex instinct to create and the destructive instinct to kill in equal measure? How could God create a father to be so cold-blooded?

As I sat in the *mandir* (temple) during *bhajans* (devotional singing), I railed against God. All the sadness of all the mothers who had lost their children over the ages flowed through me. And these kittens were not even mine. I had not adopted them as mine. And yet. . .

The only way I could let go of the pain that nature inflicts was to try to make some sense of it. When I am subjected to something that seems wholly mechanical and purposeless, I feel like a victim. My intrinsic belief in the meaningfulness and justice of a holistic, interconnected universe was being brought into question. What emerged was the following writing.

# Nature

Nature is wholly indifferent to
the plight of her inhabitants
the law of the jungle says
the weak are destroyed by the strong

as a human I could have intervened and
protected the weak. But I thought it
would be interfering with the mother's role
as protector. Am I to leave nature to
her own devices or am I to protect?

to protect is a responsibility. If done with
attachment, new *karma*[2] is deposited in
the mind bank in preparation for
future fruition. If done without attachment
it is service

I had the premonition and the cues and said,
"If only I had known this would happen
I would've invited them in and
let them grow up in my room"

then when I discovered
they were in fact alive I
somehow thought the mother should
bring them into my room of her own accord

---

2 *Karma* means action related to cause and effect. We reap what we sow. The aim is to purify the mind of conditioning formed by our past actions. Inner purification occurs when we perform actions for something higher than our own ego, while letting go of the desire for results.

I invited her in and she didn't come
it felt too imposing for me to put her
babies in my room so I didn't do it

I didn't like her dirty rooftop spot
the father loomed near. I didn't trust his
paranoid ways. When the screeching
catcalls came, little did I know
this was the call of death
the babies' guts were gouged out in blood

brutal brutal brutal was the bully of a father
as part of nature he was a killer
the raw sex instinct has
no regard for mother's milk
her heartfelt screech was her only response
to the heartless killer

what is my role in all this?
am I to be a protector or
am I to be a witness?

the best is to be a witness protector
like Vishnu[3]
ever engaged yet wholly detached

left to her own devices
nature doesn't care
creation, preservation and destruction
are all the same to her

---

3 Vishnu represents the aspect of the totality that embodies the energy of preservation. He is the god who protects humanity and allows life to continue and flourish.

her time scale is larger than
three tiny births or
maybe even six million

she is not moved by
goodness or cuteness
she can be cold as ice

but when a spark of loving
detachment is brought into the arena
nature discovers her harmony
creation as sex instinct is
no longer at odds with preservation
creation need not lead to premature death

but only under certain circumstances and
to a limited extent
some animal aggression cannot be transformed
it must be eradicated

now three little kittens
so adorable and sweet
lie buried under the earth
while nature continues

This cruel folly built into nature could only be understood as her program to keep down the cat population.

For a few days Sweetie disappeared. Then I spotted her romping with the father. How could she be with a creature who had murdered her own babies right in front of her eyes? Clearly something was going on that I could not comprehend.

Then one day she showed up at my door. I had never let her in before, but now I felt so sorry for her I allowed her to enter. And what did she do? She began searching behind every nook and cranny, behind the curtain, behind the trunks, behind the pots and pans. In the bathroom, under the sink, she searched and searched and didn't stop. I knew she was looking for her babies. I patted her gently.

"The kittens aren't here, Sweetie. They're in cat heaven." She just stood there and looked at me.

"It's a very good place for kittens. God is taking good care of them."

She ignored my words and persevered in her search.

"Sweetie. If I had known this would happen, I would've let you give birth in my place." My heart reached out to her. But little did I comprehend the seriousness of my words.

She continued her search. Only later did I know for sure that she understood me perfectly.

# 4

## IN TUNE WITH THE GODDESS

**M**eanwhile, Tom's behavior was incorrigible. One afternoon, an English friend, Joan, brought her son over to fix my computer. Shortly after leaving, this strapping six footer came running back to my room in terror. "There's a cat on the stairs. He won't let me pass. He keeps growling as if he's going to pounce."

Usually Tom ran away from people. But now something had changed. I walked out to try to help the young man down the stairs. "Go away, Tom."

He didn't budge. Even at me he just growled with disdain—a deep empowered growl, more confident than ever of his capacity to kill. Only by sprinkling water on Tom could we regain use of our territory.

I felt a big responsibility thrust upon my shoulders. If the male was a killer, shouldn't he be neutered? Then he would no longer be given the chance to kill his own kittens. It would also make him more friendly and less aggressive. But the solution wasn't that simple.

First of all, it was impossible to catch him, as he avoided people. This guy was a real paranoid cat. So we would have to put a tranquilizer in his food. Meat was off-limits in the ashram, and we couldn't put a tranquilizer in milk without him smelling it. But even more major was the question of what Sweetie would do when she went into heat. A long-time ashramite named Tara, who had been Sweetie's friend and mentor over the years, said Sweetie was so loyal to Tom that she would fight any other cat who tried to mate with her. Once she gave a potential suitor a major scratch near his eye. She only wanted Tom, also known as Maximus Rex. By neutering Tom, might we be setting up a situation of infidelity, not only in the present but in future incarnations as well, when Sweetie and Tom would be born as human beings? Clearly that would be meddling with karma, which could only lead to an unwholesome chain of consequences for the cats as well as for ourselves.

The other possibility was sterilizing Sweetie. This operation is more serious for females than for males. With sanitation as filthy as it is in India, this would mean subjecting Sweetie to the risk of infection. Besides, she really was a wonderful mother. The dharma of a female cat consists of mating, nursing, nurturing, hunting, and mating again. If we forcibly ended this cycle prematurely, would we be compelling Sweetie to take another cat birth[4] to fulfill her desire to have more kittens?

And what about all those kittens with their very short life spans? From the perspective of the body, it seems cruel that they should die so young, so often, and so brutally. A part of me really wanted to do everything possible to prevent their premature deaths. But from the vantage point of the soul, is it not possible that even a brief life span serves some hidden essential purpose—for the being itself as well as for the earth?

I do not know the answer to these questions. But I do know it didn't feel right to subject Sweetie to sterilization. She was not an indoor pet who had people to love and care for her. Her dharma was different. And it did feel important to consider the all-around well-being of these animals from as wide a perspective as possible, as if their importance as inhabitants of the kingdom of earth were equal to our own.

This inner encounter with nature caused me to reconsider my automatically liberal views regarding abortion and the right to life—not from any political or moralistic stance, but from the perspective of what feels

---

4 According to the theory of reincarnation, the soul is drawn to be born in the environment that offers the best potential for living out its desires and working through its karma.

right inside, in accordance with nature. And I came to see that one thing that distinguishes human beings from animals is the possibility for real freedom of choice—for oneself alone. It is simply not right for us to arbitrarily impose our own values on other people or on animals. For our ways are not always wiser than Mother Nature's. My individual nature was to become a full embodiment of Mother Nature and live in harmony with her law—that I might help the will of the Goddess live on earth. My inner sensitivity was to be applied to every aspect of my life. Only this way, could I possibly live in Truth.

# 5

## THE JOY OF CHILDBIRTH

Time was passing quickly. Sweetie's belly was getting larger. We thought the kittens would be born in November, but we were wrong. The gestation period for a cat is only two months, not three. By now Sweetie was spoiled rotten. I let her into my room every evening and fed her milk or curd. I petted her. She purred. Then she would walk around a bit and go sit in a few favorite spots. She especially liked the blue-and-white mat behind the closet curtain. Then I would chant some Sanskrit verses and prayers, while Sweetie would sit on the floor near my chair and listen intently. I let her stay for about an hour. When it was time for her to go, she unwillingly acquiesced. I would pat her, carry her out, and close the door.

One night, however, something very different occurred. Instead of sitting quietly, Sweetie began pacing frantically and shoved her plump body into every nook and cranny. Behind the trunk, under the bed, on the shelf, in the pots and pans, under the sink, in the box, she walked and walked to and fro as if she were looking for something. By now I surely knew how inscrutable was cat behavior. I also stopped trying to make sense of the unexpected, even though my mind kept trying. Whenever an unwanted thought appeared I simply let it go by, not giving it any attention. In this way, my automatic mental processes would gradually fizzle out, making room for something deeper to emerge. Our inner evaluator can be very good at separating gold from garbage, wheat from the chaff—sometimes. Other times, we believe what the limited mind tells us and misperceptions take over!

If I hadn't been told the cat's gestation period was three months, I would have assumed that this idiosyncratic feline was looking for a spot to give birth. But only two months had gone by since that fateful day when Sweetie and Tom went romping.

When I tried to take Sweetie out of my room, something unusual happened. She hissed at me. I tried to pick her up again. She scratched. "Sweetie, what happened to you?" I asked.

She was showing me her wild nature as a cat, even though her disposition was usually very sweet and cooperative. I had to wrap her in a towel to carry her out, or else she would have refused to budge. All night long, she slept on the chair on the veranda outside my door.

Early the next morning I heard her howling. It was a wild and adamant howl. I had no choice but to let her in.

She walked into the kitchen and sat herself down right in the middle of the shelf with the pots and pans. And she began purring and purring. I looked at her. She was perpetually smiling. Something special was happening. Louder and louder she purred, to the beat of some invisible rhythm. Her presence was wondrous. Her joy was contagious.

Sweetie always was a contented cat, but I had never witnessed anything like this! It felt as if the Great Goddess herself was sitting in the middle of my kitchen.

At about 6:30 A.M. I left for *darshan*.[5] A couple of hours later when I returned, I entered the kitchen. There behind a great big box, on top of a crinkly piece of plastic, something squeaked. It was a tiny newborn kitten. Before long another one emerged. The miracle of creation was occurring before my very eyes!

---

5 *Darshan* means "seeing" in Sanskrit. In this context, it connotes a formal gathering when people meet to see the guru, who is considered an embodiment of God.

What mystical bliss this mother experienced during childbirth. Just one tiny yelp. No pain. Total relaxation and receptivity to the joy of creation, the joy of life, the oneness of the universe.

She licked the babies. I brought her some milk. I sent them love. And the feeding cycle had begun.

This time she let me know for sure that she didn't want me watching. She gave me a really dirty look whenever I glanced her way. Beyond words, her eyes communicated unequivocally, "No." Clearly, like most nursing mothers during their intimate moments, this cat wanted her privacy. No distractions, no intrusions—only the cat nourishing her kittens in full concentration and containment.

I lifted the lid of the box to screen out unwelcome glances and gave the new family their own private space under the counter in the midst of my kitchen.

# 6

## THE UNEXPECTED

The first two weeks of kitten life were miraculous and contained. Everything was left to the mom, and I didn't do a thing except enjoy their wondrous presence. I was a simple, loving witness to the miracle of life. But how long could I remain a witness without being drawn into the nitty-gritty of daily life issues?

Every morning before dawn Sweetie would leave to go hunting. The first few times she returned promptly to resume her feeding, which was almost continuous. But soon, she began to enjoy her freedom. One day, it seemed as if she had forgotten to come back. Hours passed. Nine o'clock, ten o'clock. No Sweetie. She had been out since 4:00 A.M. How long could the babies survive without receiving their mother's milk?

Although Sweetie had already demonstrated her unquestionable expertise in mothering skills, I was still very anxious. Was she dopey enough to forget? Did she fall asleep under a tree or chase a frog unto infinity? Or did she just go romping with Tom and lose all track of time?

As my anxiety mounted, I recalled what Sai Baba had said to me during my first interview, ten years before: "You worry too much. You worry too much."

Yes. It was still true. I worried too much. When faith in the order of events is total, there is no need for anxiety. There is no need for worry.

There is only acceptance—acceptance of the love permeating everything, no matter what. This is reality. But I wasn't there yet.

Before long, I checked with my friend Tara, the compassionate protector of animal life. At one time, she had provided food and shelter to nine cats of several generations, as well as dogs, monkeys, and pigeons. "No, Sweetie's not here," she said. "Don't worry. She'll be back."

I gazed at the kittens. They were fast asleep, peacefully intertwined with one another. From time to time they woke up and started sucking and searching for the breast. When they couldn't find it, they went back to sleep.

I needed to go out to go shopping. But as my room did not come equipped with a cat door, I waited for Sweetie. Had I been foolish enough to leave the door open, the first animal to enter would probably have been Tom—with potentially disastrous results. Monkeys were also likely to pay an uninvited visit, as were mosquitoes, bees, and all sorts of other biting creatures. No. In spite of my impatience, I was forced to stay at home and wait.

At 11:00 A.M. she finally showed up. I reprimanded her for her tardiness. She made a beeline for the babies. They were starving and devoured her milk. This time no licking was necessary to stimulate their desire to drink.

Slowly but surely, I could see myself being drawn into this cat family. Even their habits and instincts were being interpreted from my human perspective. Why was it so difficult for me to just be detached and let well enough alone?

After about a week, Sweetie let me know it was okay for me to watch the kittens during mealtime. When I peeked, no more dirty looks. So I put down the lid of the box. And what did I see? The little gray-and-white striped one hogged the breast. He thrust his entire body to cover up all the nipples, so the little black-and-white one was unable to eat. Again, Sweetie did not do a thing. The tiny black-and-white kitten was decidedly smaller than the gray-and-white striper. Now I understood why. She had to overcome grave obstructions to the food supply.

This time I intervened. I moved the tiny gray-and-white body out of the parallel position that covered Sweetie's entire chest. I showed the hungry kitten he could drink very nicely at right angles to Sweetie. All he needed was one nipple—not the whole belly! Then I guided the little black-and-white one to the breast. She seemed so relieved. She was famished!

But was it okay for me to touch the kittens? Left to her own devices in nature, the little black-and-white infant might have died of starvation. So the tiny twinge of guilt that I felt for my interference with nature did not stop me from helping. Later, when I consulted the vet, he corroborated that it was fine for me to guide a kitten to the breast as needed.

As I began to feel more comfortable handling the babies, and neither they nor the mother seemed to mind, the time seemed right to confirm important issues of gender identity. Were they really a gray-striped boy and a black-striped girl? This information was essential in the naming process.

First I turned over the little black-and-white one. And what did I see? A little round dot. To my amazement, "she" was a boy. Then, when I inspected the little gray-and-white striper, "he" turned out to be a girl! The one who carried the mother's markings was a boy, and the one who looked like dad was a girl. The more assertive one was a girl, and the more passive one was a boy. Around this cat species, the only surety is the unexpected!

I wanted to give them names that would suit their personalities, so I carefully observed their behavior. The gray one was a bundle of dynamite, in constant motion, ever wiggling around to make her way to the breast. She often stepped on her brother, walked on him, got on top of him. Yet, he didn't seem to react or feel intruded upon one bit. He simply remained peaceful and even-tempered under all circumstances. So I named the girl Vritti, which means "movement" in Sanskrit. And I called the boy Samah, which means "equal-minded."

Before long, Vritti's behavior changed. Instead of pushing her brother and stepping on him, she started putting her arm around him, hugging him, and licking him lovingly. So I changed her name to Bhakti, which means "devotion." After all, it's a terrible thing to go through life with a name like Vritti! Samah's behavior also changed very drastically, but that was much later, and by that time it was too late to change his name. For now the new babies were officially called Bhakti Vritti Baba and Samah Tushti Baba. *Tushti* means "contentment."

Around this time, a thought flashed through my mind: *Samah is my father. Bhakti is my grandmother.* "Where did that come from?" I wondered. Then I realized that my father embodied the calm, steady temperament of Samah. He was extremely good natured and remained unperturbed under the most difficult circumstances. And my grandmother was the embodiment of unconditional love and devotion to others. The thought registered for a moment. And then I forgot about it until much later in our story.

My life of peaceful loving wonder continued. But unbeknownst to me, it would be short-lived.

# 7

## THE UNIVERSE EXPANDS

**M**uch of the time in my room was spent observing Sweetie and the kittens, sending them love and receiving their love. Sweetie's mothering skills were utterly superb. She performed her dharma with total concentration, total loyalty, and total love. Her whole being supported her every action. With the maturing of the kittens, her repertoire of behaviors expanded, but never did her excellence waver. For now, her duty consisted primarily of licking both kittens to prod them to suckle, so they would receive the nourishment they needed to grow and thrive.

To my surprise, now Sweetie licked Bhakti more than Samah. She really had to work on Bhakti to encourage her to eat. With Samah it was different. With one or two licks, he would be at the breast immediately. Individual differences, our distinct personalities, are present from birth. All conditioning is just superimposed onto the essential qualities of a being, whether cat or human.

Before long, the babies started learning to walk. They were a bit wobbly at first, but no longer did they need to slither and crawl amongst the crinkly plastic. They walked upright from the green mat to the red striped towel, and back again from the towel to the mat. Sometimes they stepped on each other. The mother watched happily and let them be.

Then one day I noticed something very disturbing. Samah's left eye remained closed. What if Bhakti had stepped on his eye? Could her sharp claws do irreparable damage to his sight? For a long time I watched. His eye still remained closed. If he were blind in one eye, how could he survive? It was difficult enough for a healthy cat to thrive in the wild, let alone an injured one. I felt really bad. Here I was, worrying again.

The next morning the eye was still closed. Sadly I thought, "I'll have to go to the vet." But miraculously, in the afternoon, Samah's eye was wide open.

Meanwhile, a modus vivendi had to be arranged for Sweetie's calls of nature, as I wasn't always there to let her out as needed. The outdoor soil, which I placed in the dish bin on the floor near the sink was to be her new litter box. Although she had always lived in the wild, Sweetie caught on very quickly to the ins and outs of feline domesticity. But the wet soil stuck to her belly and turned out to be quite unsanitary for the nursing babies.

Once the litter box was disposed of, Sweetie somehow knew I didn't want her stuff all over my kitchen, or even in her towel. So what do you think this marvelous creature did? Completely on her own, totally untaught, she went into the bathroom and defecated into the drain hole of the shower. What intelligence! What consideration! Sweetie was filled with wondrous surprises.

By now, Bhakti and Samah were becoming energized with the joy of mobility. What had once been their entire world was beginning to expand. Now the kingdom of mother, sibling, towel, mat, and crinkly plastic also began to include the box—especially the wall of the box. It was meant for climbing!

Bhakti took the lead. Samah followed. Up and up she went, but couldn't yet make it to the top. Next they learned pushing and squeezing through the gap, so as to discover a whole new room called the kitchen. No longer could I keep them contained in their peaceful little universe. It was time to let go. My tranquil days were soon coming to an end. There was a great big world out there waiting to be discovered. My task was to be alert enough not to step on them.

At first they shyly made their way around the room—sometimes in circles. Before long, they made a beeline for the refrigerator. It was propped up on a plastic dolly. Under it they went. Not only did they like hidden places, they loved warm places. And Indian refrigerators generate lots of heat! Unfortunately, it comes from the grill in the back, and Bhakti almost got stuck there between the metal casing and the body of the fridge. Although I tried to train them not to go there, it was impossible. They loved it. So warm and contained and secure. Don't we too often also love what is not good for us?

My next task was to construct a cardboard wall and tape it to the fridge so the kittens would not get stuck there or get electrocuted.

The day the kittens were born, I was to leave for a dentist appointment in Bangalore. Some time before, while traveling in the Himalayas, I had lost a huge filling. The tooth undoubtedly needed a cap. Then, for one reason or another, the appointment kept getting postponed. Somehow, the timing never seemed right. And after the kittens were born, I certainly was not about to leave them for a few days just to see the dentist!

Now after a couple of weeks, the cat family felt perfectly at home. Sweetie was comfortable enough not only to leave her babies alone with me, but also to allow a couple of my friends close enough to observe them. Lisa was a real cat person. I invited her over to see the kittens. They were not afraid, and she got along very well with Sweetie. When I saw them interacting together, I knew I had found the perfect babysitter. Lisa was delighted at the idea of spending some alone time in my room with the cat family.

Before leaving for Bangalore, I left instructions regarding boiling the fresh cow milk for Sweetie. My main concern was that Lisa should be at home when Sweetie returned from hunting. There was nothing to worry about. Everything would be fine.

Three days later, I returned from my dentist appointment in a van that was transporting some nicely wrapped new furniture for my room. Would you believe that the kittens had grown decidedly larger in just three days—not only physically but psychologically as well? They had now discovered the broom, the dustpan, and the laundry bag. They scooted up the broom handle, which was resting on the laundry bag, then they scooted down the broom into the dustpan. If the angle was right, this dual contraption served as a kind of seesaw that popped up when they placed their weight on the broom head that rested on top of the handle of the dustpan. After scurrying back and forth with all these toys, the kittens would soon fall asleep, exhausted, on top of the laundry bag, which was very well padded—as it was usually full.

# 8

## THE HEALERS

Soon I learned that in addition to being fun and wondrous, the kittens were also healers. And they didn't have to do anything in particular—just be themselves. When Lisa was a young mother, she chanced upon a little black-and-white kitten, whom she named Willie. She found him in bad shape in the garbage pail, abandoned by his mother. Then she nursed him back to health. But as it turned out, Lisa felt compelled to give Willie away because he couldn't be litter-trained. As she had a crawling infant on the floor, it was too unsanitary to subject the baby to kitten droppings. Although she had found a good home for Willie, she felt she had never really said good-bye. And to make matters worse, he later died, purportedly of a "broken heart."

Samah looked just like Willie. Being in his presence served to help Lisa bring an incomplete and painful event to a healthy sense of closure. The love and fun they shared together helped not only Lisa, but also the kittens.

As a playful problem-solving exercise, Lisa arranged the boxes into a multilevel mazelike structure, where the kittens could crawl from one box to the next and run up and down to their hearts' content. And at such a young age they even wrestled, priming their muscles and ligaments for the days ahead when fighting would no longer be fun, but a matter of survival. Bhakti always took the lead. Whatever she did Samah would copy. Later on, when Samah became bigger than Bhakti, all that would change. But for now, the spicy little girl was the dominant one.

Their play space on the kitchen floor was like heaven—good and beautiful, with never a dull moment. Even Sweetie participated in the play. She loved moving her tail back and forth while the kittens tried to grab it. They never quite seemed to be quick enough! Yet they never stopped trying. *To be alert enough to catch the uncatchable in less than a split second is the ongoing secret of spirituality.*

These were very happy moments and still not too much trouble. Yes, as time went by I was washing more towels, as a little defecation had begun. Yet they still had their space and I had mine, and life was contented and easy.

But the threat of the father loomed heavy in the background. Tom was forever keeping tabs on them. Every night he came by, sometimes sneakily and sometimes overtly meowing for Sweetie. If she didn't come out, he would go behind the building near the shaft space and howl. This often happened while she was breast-feeding. Then she would get upset and want to leave. When she left, she sometimes wouldn't return till twelve or two in the morning. Then she would meow and meow at the door until she woke me up and I was compelled to let her in. This cat had dogged perseverance! I was being forced to accommodate and adapt to her needs.

At first, I took it as a spiritual training in learning flexibility, acceptance, and detachment from the body. But as time went on, I became more and more tired. I really didn't like having my sleep disturbed. I was never one of those people who willingly pulled all-nighters in college.

In spite of minor annoyances, I knew full well that if I accepted the dharma of being a foster mother to a cat family, I also had to accept the bad with the good. Just because their cat ways might be annoying, it was unthinkable for me to send them away. It simply wasn't right. With horror, I recalled all the stray animals who are abandoned because their owners leave town or lose interest when the going gets rough. I was not going to participate in such a hurtful form of narcissism!

All beings have an equal right to life, liberty, and the pursuit of happiness. If Sweetie's pursuit of happiness conflicted with mine, I would have to adapt, as I was from a more advanced species. Or was I?

As time went on, I came to see that this partnership was not controlled by me, though I might have fooled myself into thinking I was taking care of them. It was in fact Sweetie and the kittens who were taking care of me. Whatever I needed in order to grow out of my limited skin was being presented to me. The Great Goddess, the Divine Mother, was overseeing my inner development through the vehicle of this wondrous cat family. And this was only the beginning!

# 9

## THE ILLUSION OF "MY SPACE"

During these early days, I had one overriding fear regarding kitten safety—the father. Although I had adopted the infants out of empathy for Sweetie and to give them the chance to live, I questioned Sweetie's intelligence on this score. Did she really know about the murders of her kittens, or had she blocked it all out? And if she did know, would her natural instinct to keep moving baby kittens prove stronger than her intelligence? In short, I was afraid Sweetie would try to take the kittens out and then the father would kill them.

I consulted the vet regarding this concern. Though he had a very good heart and loved animals, he knew little about cat behavior. In general, he felt it would be safer to keep them out of reach of the father till they were two months old and had been weaned. I deduced that the father had repeatedly killed litters of Sweetie's babies over the years, as Tara revealed that only a couple of her kittens had survived. The instinctive motivation for the killings seemed to be sex and envy. When Sweetie was busy nursing and spending all her time with babies, would Tom not wish to get rid of them? This cat had sex on the brain! Sweetie's fertility and loyalty seemed to attest to his masculine prowess as well as his ability to keep her happy. But after all, the joy of sex has its limits—even in a cat!

Sweetie was getting restless. She paced around the room. If she tried to take out the kittens, I would distract her. What if it made her depressed to stay indoors with them, as she was by nature a wild cat getting on in years? Would the imprint of wild cat mothering behaviors prove stronger than her simple common sense?

In all the time she remained in my room, never once did I see her lift the babies. When they were old enough to walk, they simply followed her. I remained alert to future possibilities and watched.

By now their world was expanding again. A major leap out of the kitchen into the living room was in order. I dreaded this moment with cringes of foreboding, though I had no real idea about the degree of wild chaos that was soon to enter my living space. But the Goddess is good. It all happens slowly and in spurts, to give us the opportunity to adapt.

Bhakti stood on the threshold of the kitchen doorway and looked. She soon turned around and returned to the security of the kitchen. After a time she came again to this spot. Then Samah ventured out. Bhakti followed. First they walked around and began to explore. Then they began to run and wrestle. The room was a great place to play tag and cat hide-and-seek. Behind the trunk, over the mattress, on top of the altar—no place was sacrosanct. I tried to train them to stay off my mattress, but it was extremely difficult.

Soon they had completely taken over "my space." But was not the concept of "my space" an illusion created by needs of the body and ego? The reality of territoriality is for animals, not human beings. If I choose to overstep the order of nature by inviting animals into my home, I must learn not only to share and accept, but also to transcend.

After all, kittens will be kittens. I didn't want to squelch their spirit. And viewed from a higher level, we are all equal children of the Goddess, each with our own individual part to play. From this angle, no one species is better than another, just as no one person is better than another, based on intelligence, skills, or profession.

Sweetie soon showed Bhakti and Samah how to use my new desk as a scratching post. Fortunately, I had left the paper wrapping on, especially for them. Am I glad I did!

With Bhakti, climbing came as naturally as breathing. She had been first to climb over the box into the kitchen. Again she led the way, climbing up the legs of my new desk. After several tries, she finally made it to the top. Samah followed. The new desk with all its paper wrappings now became as important a play spot as the laundry bag. I found myself forever sweeping up bits and pieces of paper. The wrapping was being torn to shreds by their sharp claws. And how Samah loved biting paper! Though I feared my new desk might be developing scratches before its first use, I didn't really mind. I thought I was developing patience.

Soon Bhakti discovered the long cotton curtains, which served as closet doors. Up and up she climbed till she made it to the top. Seven feet up, above the curtains, was a ledge for storage. She somehow managed to get up there, but really didn't like it. She wanted to come down, but couldn't. She started meowing and crying.

I stood on a chair and tried to help her down, but she ran farther and farther back where it was impossible to reach her. What to do? I let her be. But there was no way she could climb down. Finally, I managed to catch her and carry her down.

It was quite surprising for me to see that, intrinsically, the little girl had a more adventurous spirit than the boy. Kitten observation corroborated that many of our stereotyped ideas about gender identity are really culturally conditioned and not biologically determined—at least in the beginning, before childbearing years. Still, we cannot underestimate the potency of the animal brain in human beings, as it remains the basis for much of our motivation and behavior. In some ways it beats cultural conditioning—depending on the "culture." At times, our animal heritage of territoriality and survival of the fittest (the euphemism used for being a self-centered bully) automatically rules our psyche and prevents more compassionate behavior from manifesting. But with the kittens, everything seemed to fit together and reveal its own spontaneous natural order. This is not always the case with us human beings, as the mind presents us with so many veils, conflicts, and interferences.

It was around this time that I gave the kittens their first oral spiritual teachings. They had already experienced the vibrations of meditation and

Sanskrit chanting, but never before had they been exposed to what is commonly known as a "sermon." They were sitting on top of the desk looking at me with perfect openness and love. I petted them. They purred.

"Now, kittens. You are very close to God. You are filled with love. You are very smart, so I know you'll understand everything I say." Although I had no doubt that these kittens already knew everything I was about to tell them, nonetheless it felt important for me to share my thoughts with them and play my human role to the best of my ability. Surely they already understood their true origin, their true ancestry—beyond their particular mother and father.[6] Still I continued to participate in the game.

"Always be good kittens. Always follow your cat dharma. Do exactly what you were meant to do in this life. Be exactly what you were meant to be."

They looked at me so lovingly, so contentedly. Then they gazed at each other with a smile, as if to acknowledge that they were receiving something of great value, and it was fully understood. They looked at me again with total receptivity.

"You are wonderful kittens. God loves you very much. I love you very much. Continue to be the wonderful kittens that you are. And God will always be with you." Amen.

The kittens eyed each other once more in undeniable acknowledgment of their chosenness under God. And they resumed their play.

Several days passed before Bhakti tried climbing the curtain again. Again, a repeat performance. If only I could have trained her to climb down, it would have saved her a lot of suffering and trauma in the future. But everything happens in its time. Don't we all know that, in some areas, parents simply cannot teach their children what is necessary to save them from suffering? For it may be that suffering is exactly what is needed to help us work through our karma and expand. As for Samah, he wasn't yet interested in climbing curtains.

---

6 The sixth sense attributed to cats, I feel, stems from their affinity with nature, without the constricting divisions of past, present, and future that the human mind imposes. The true continuous ancestry of all beings, according to Vedanta philosophy, is both immanent Mother Nature and transcendent Father God (*Mula Prakriti* and the Supreme *Purusha*).

# 10

## THE ILLUSION OF THE SACRED
## AND THE MUNDANE

During the day, the kittens had free rein of the living room. Only at night did I tuck them into bed behind the box and close the kitchen door. At first, this worked out okay. But Sweetie was restless. She didn't like being cooped up in the kitchen at night. So she began jumping on the door, thumping on the door, banging on the door, and dropping the kitchen utensils on the floor. I finally opened it and let her into the living room. This sweet little fat cat knew how to get exactly what she wanted—and all without the use of language. *The most persuasive messages are nonverbal.*

Foolishly I explained to Sweetie, as if it were my choice, "You can stay here as long as you are quiet. I don't want you stepping on me or coming onto my mattress. Find a nice spot on one of your mats and sleep well."

She walked around a bit and parked herself right next to my bed. This was too close for comfort, as I slept on the floor, and I surely didn't want her waking me up in the middle of the night. So I patted her, picked her up, and put her on the mat behind the closet curtain. "Remember, no cat naps and meows."

I thought she got the message, as miraculously she managed to sleep through the night till 3:30 A.M. And so did I. If ever I might have needed an alarm clock to rise before dawn, that need had now totally vanished. I opened the kitchen door and Sweetie went in to feed the babies. Then she went out to hunt. In a flash, Bhakti and Samah came racing into the living room. Their games of tag made it very difficult for me to do my meditation. For as part of the chase, they ran over me as if I were nothing but furniture. Some people have no sense of personal space and treat others like objects, but believe me, kittens are worse!

As it turned out, this was the very issue my teacher, Sweetie/Sai Baba,[7] was helping me to work on—with such love and caring. How could the illusory notion of ego, of "I" and "my" ever dissolve without living the experience in the nitty-gritty of everyday life? It was one thing to experience this in meditation, or to know intellectually that I am not the body and I am not the mind, and I am not my actions or my talents, or my likes and dislikes. But it was something else to be, to simply *be*, to rest in my true nature, a loving space of energized consciousness—no matter what. Only then would I not react to intrusion both external and internal. Only then would I truly earn the right to be called nonviolent. My preconceived notions regarding what was "holy" and what was "non-holy" had to go. For everything is holy.

If you think I was being hard on myself, you are not correct. This ashram is not an easy school. True learning requires struggle and not just mental magic. I was well aware that it was natural and human for me to have an emotional reaction to intrusion. But what I was aiming at was to be able to live in the ongoing awareness that something higher is ever supporting all my actions and reactions. *When I could be in touch with this exquisite awareness, all my emotional reactions would be subsumed into loving consciousness.* It wouldn't matter what activity I participated in, as no one thing is any better than another. Then all the transient happenings and pinpricks of life would not for a moment be seen as real, would not for a second be experienced as all there is. Something more inclusive, more of the essence of existence, much deeper than simply the daily unfolding of events, would always live with me, no matter what.

---

7 All beings, and events, as part of the universal cosmic form of God, can serve as our teachers, since all things exude a spark of the oneness of life.

Call it the oneness of everything, call it infinity, call it the witness that makes no distinctions between outer and inner, call it the eternal, call it bliss, call it love. The names do not matter. If I could live in this space always everywhere, then none of the ripples on the sea would ever touch me. I would never again think in terms of self-centered interest. I would always be a force for good, no matter what the activity. And the world would be a very different place.

# 11

## PATIENCE, PATIENCE
## JUST OUT OF REACH

ll too soon, Bhakti and Samah became discontented sleeping all alone without their mom. They too wanted to go into the living room. Then they also started jumping on the kitchen door. "Little kittens. Be quiet and go to sleep."

I ignored all further noise. It worked for one or two nights. But their cat perseverance proved stronger than my human variety. As the racket continued, I felt compelled to open the door. Maybe they would sleep quietly on the floor behind the curtain.

After a few games of cat tag and some hearty wrestling, I tucked in the little ruffians on the mat behind the curtain. Many cats like to go into boxes to sleep. At this time, Bhakti and Samah did not. They used boxes for play and rest, but rarely for a good night's sleep.

Early the next morning, I was awakened by kittens running all over me. They were so sweet and cute and loving. I began petting them. Before long, there was something wet and brown and squishy in my bed.

What a thing to wake up to! Now my patience was wearing thin. But I worked very hard to control myself. As I didn't know who the culprit was, I lifted both of them up and put them on the newspaper on the kitchen floor and told them in a firm but nice way that bed was not the place for that kind of stuff. Then I washed my sheets.

A couple of days later when the same thing happened again, I completely lost my cool. This time I started yelling at them when I placed them on the newspaper. Would you believe this was the last time they ever defecated in my bed? They were actually becoming paper-trained and plastic-trained. Sometimes they peed on plastic bags that were not meant to be toilets, but that was okay. Samah's favorite bathroom was the dustpan. At least it was contained.

These kittens were brilliant! They really learned very quickly. And they were so loving and trusting and adorable. How foolish of me to be angry at them for being what they were meant to be.

In spite of ripples on the water, life was still sweet and contented. For the first time in my life, I began to feel like part of a family. In this incarnation, I had never had a positive experience of family life, of sharing, peaceful support, and give and take. Neither had I lived through the experience of being a physical mother and bringing up children. The loving aspects of my maternal nature found expression elsewhere, beyond the hassles and responsibilities of parenthood.

Maybe I had been through all that before in past lives, and there was no more need for me to repeat the whole experience again. Maybe the kittens were sent to tie up loose ends or burn up some of the seed causes of family karma, so that the cycle could be completed in as swift a way as possible, without forming new attachments. Who knows? Whatever the reasons, I did know the kittens had come to me for a purpose and I was to enjoy my time with them, which was chock-full of enormous love as well as aggravating difficulties.

# 12

## LETTING GO

The time had come once again for the universe to expand. Whenever Sweetie meowed to go out, the kittens tried to follow. Bhakti managed to escape once, but fortunately I caught her and returned her to safety immediately. As I still felt nervous about the danger of their potential exposure to the father, I kept them indoors for a while longer. But soon they became more and more persistent and tried to sneak through the door whenever it was opened, so I decided to take my cues from them. Nature's timing knows best. It wasn't right for me to squelch their instinctive wish to explore. So I called on God to protect them and opened the door.

Out they dashed! A little to the right, a little to the left, and straight ahead toward the unenclosed drop over the fourth-floor veranda. Although my plants were there shielding the drop in front of my room, the kittens were so tiny they could easily squeeze in between. And on both sides of the plants, extending over a hundred feet, was sheer open space.

I watched. They were totally ecstatic in their newly found freedom. You can just imagine what being outdoors means to a genetically wild kitten. Whenever they got too close to the edge I would pick them up and move them.

"No. No. No. Don't go there. There's a great big drop. No."

After they had run around and wrestled for a time, I saw Samah standing near the edge. He was looking down in awe at the world below. His acute gaze surveyed everyone and everything. What was really passing through his tiny little head and expansive consciousness I could only surmise. But to me, he looked like a yogi, extremely aware, witnessing the world go by. Granted, I might have been reading too much into his detached and wondrous little look. But at least I knew for certain that he was now safe from the danger of falling off the fourth-floor ledge.

A few days later, I saw Bhakti standing near the edge surveying the scene as Samah had done. What a relief!

As soon as I watered the plants, the little explorers rushed into the pots to drink. For some reason, they didn't like water in a bowl nearly as much as water in soil. But the plant fertilizer present in the soil might not be good for them. *For every joy, an opposing obstacle seems to present itself.*

Bhakti and Samah loved to climb on the plant pots and bite the leaves. Though I felt bad for the plants, I personally didn't mind that they tore the leaves to shreds. However, I did cringe when I saw them peeing in my newly planted lettuce seeds imported from Italy—seeds that I felt so fortunate to have been given. Peeing in itself wasn't a problem. Digging up the soil to cover it up with their sharp claws was the issue. Bye-bye lettuce for this year anyway!

The next step in their territorial expansion was the roof. This was Sweetie's favorite spot. Unfortunately, it was also the father's. Here the mother cat stayed safely protected from aggressive broomsticks and humans with their unpredictable ill will. It was also a haven from bullock carts, big barking dogs, and occasional cars, which were now becoming more prominent on this once pollution-free ashram. With a rooftop view of unimpeded blue sky, here Sweetie spent many happy days soaking up the sun and resting after the rigors of the chase for food. Many happy evenings she spent here with Tom doing whatever married couples do together. Now Sweetie was introducing the next generation to this hallowed spot. And I was scared.

Bhakti and Samah followed her up the stairs to the fifth-floor landing. Surprisingly enough, jumping up stairs came naturally to them.

When they walked too close to the edge, I moved them over. Soon they noticed the big drop into the stairwell and acted accordingly. In spite of momentary lapses of judgment when the joy of wrestling took over, they were usually alert to this danger.

They walked past the fifth-floor landing where the murders had occurred and followed their mom to the door, which was always locked. Fortunately, there was about a six-inch space under the door. Sweetie slithered through. The kittens followed.

I said good-bye with joyful acceptance combined with a little heaviness of heart. For I knew Tom wasn't there now, but what about later? This was his favorite haunt when the sun went down. Would Sweetie be swift enough to protect the babies from his murderous instincts? Though this was only a temporary and brief good-bye, it was the first time they had been out without my presence. It would have been impossible for me to slither through the six-inch gap under the door. I had to learn to trust in Providence and let go.

So I tried to go about my business, but the kittens were forever on my mind. When it was time for lunch, I went up there again to call. "Sweetie, Bhakti, Samah. It's time for lunch."

To my great surprise, they emerged in an instant. We greeted each other joyfully, exchanged lots of love and petting. They followed me back down the stairs. I guess I too was being imprinted in their psyches as mother, alongside Sweetie. And she also was imprinting me as a quasi-authority figure, while maintaining no doubt in her mind about who was really in charge!

Sometimes Sweetie brought the babies back on her own initiative. Other times she lingered there with them too long for comfort. Sometimes they came out when I called. Other times they did not. It felt imperative for me to get the key to the roof. Once this precious piece of metal was in my possession, I rested much easier.

# 13

## MOTHERING WITHOUT STRESS

The first time Sweetie took the kittens to the roof in the evening, I was really scared. For I knew the father would be around. As it was, he always managed to keep tabs on their whereabouts. Almost every night, he would walk by the veranda outside my room to call Sweetie or just sniff and see if the kittens were still there. Like a private detective, he knew everything that was going on. What was his purpose in all this? Was it malevolent or neutral? Did he just want to romp with Sweetie, or was he also plotting to kill the babies?

Since natural events seemed to be taking their course in spite of my protective instincts and reservations, I just had to go along with nature—but in a way that brought in a spark of intelligence and alertness. The give and take that is required in being a good mother is remarkable. You have to be supple as the branches of the weeping willow tree that flows with the breezes, and still bring shade.

Sweetie was a superb mother. She let her babies do whatever came naturally. She never said "No." She was 100 percent there for them, watching and silently encouraging, but never interfering. And they did whatever was right for them. Mother Nature would protect them in harmony with her plan. Cat mothering did not entail adding anything preferential or unnecessary to Mother Nature. It was all one. Nothing was superimposed.

Sweetie's actions were fully in tune with the divine plan. All results were dictated by a higher power. No ego had yet entered the arena. Whatever "mind" was present was a perfect reflection of Mother Nature.

This mother fully enjoyed her kittens. No one duty was better than another. Everything was equally important. Whether she was breast-feeding or taking them out or moving her tail back and forth, she gave it her all, without any like or dislike. She took everything as it came, without looking for specific results.

Bhakti and Samah invented a game, which they taught Sweetie how to play. The long strap from my pocketbook hung down from the table. The kittens would jump up and hit it; back and forth, back and forth, it would move until, eventually, the bag might be dragged to the floor. Sweetie watched with an attentive smile on her face. She too walked over to play. The freedom and spontaneity that came from living this way were magical and stressless. But even this philosophy has its drawbacks, when viewed from the all-too-human perspective of valuing life. The pocketbook game might be safe for them, but what about nights on the roof?

Only when you begin thinking in terms of saving a life, does worry enter the scene. The question then becomes: Do you trust God or Goddess enough to let them take care of life, or do you feel compelled to intervene?

Intervention alone need not bring stress, but usually the motivation to help turns into taking responsibility for the outcome. *The results are simply not in our hands alone.* Human effort is always coupled with a host of other factors such as the other people's or cats' karma—if in fact cats do accumulate karma. So once we start wishing for our effort to bear fruit, this brings stress. Although I was very much aware of these factors, it was still difficult for me not to be attached to the kittens. I really wanted them to live and thrive, and felt I would do everything possible to help them. Was it humanly possible for me to love them and help them without being attached?

The moment I had been dreading finally arrived. Sweetie took the kittens to the roof in the evening. I asked God to protect them and let them be, but not without my usual share of anxiety. After a while, I would go up to the roof and check them out.

I brought a flashlight, which proved unnecessary, as the moonlight sufficed to allow acute vision. I turned the key in the lock. The silence felt holy. I turned the corner to the left side of the roof. What did I see? About halfway down near the edge sat Sweetie and the kittens. And about ten feet away sat Tom!

"Hi, Sweetie. Hi, Bhakti. Hi, Samah. Hi, Tom." I cringed in fear. "Would you kittens like to come home now?"

They all just looked at me.

"Tom. You're a good boy. I'm glad to see you're making friends with your babies."

My words had a hollow ring, as I doubted their veracity. But maybe it was really possible. Could his attitude really be undergoing a change?

Something about this atmosphere felt very unusual, unbelievably special. Then I realized why. On the floor next to Sweetie and the kittens was a dead bird, half-eaten. Sweetie was initiating them into the ritual of hunting, in the presence of the father! After all, they were a family. And killer or not, he too wanted to participate.

I stood there in utter awe. It felt as if I was witnessing something primordial, ancient, archetypal, and utterly sacred. All I can say is that the vibrations felt similar to darshan, or to the mass. In a flash, the first supper and the Last Supper somehow came together. Time, as we know it, had vanished. Silently I stood watching, drinking in the magic. Total stillness permeated the air. The act of the hunt and the act of eating became demonstrably sacred acts. The holiness of animal ritual proved fully equal to the holiness of human ritual. *The ongoing sacrifice of nature to feed animal life is as sacred a rite as the ongoing sacrifice of Christ to nourish the human soul.* And my participation in this wondrous moment of inclusion in the mystery of life was made possible by four members of the cat species!

Before long, in awesome stillness, I turned around to depart and left them to their feast.

# 14

## THE MONGOOSE

Was it possible that Tom was no longer a threat to the kittens? They couldn't have been more than four or five weeks old at the time, and were as yet far from being weaned. Since the vet had said the danger was present until they were weaned, I knew that I must still remain cautious.

Sweetie now began taking the kittens outside. Down the stairs they walked, following their mother. When they stopped or were sidetracked toward the corridors, I would help Sweetie by catching the wanderer and bringing the kitten back. Sometimes it was Bhakti, sometimes Samah. But eventually, they both finally made it to the bottom. I lingered behind and watched. She led them in back of the building, where nature was pristine and wild. Of course, even there they didn't exactly follow. One might wait behind, the other might go off on his own. Now their safety was in her hands—with God's help. They turned the corner. I lost sight of them.

Late in the afternoon, Sweetie returned without the babies. She began scurrying around the room as if she were looking for them. It seemed as if they were lost. I fed her. "Sweetie," I said. "Where are the kittens?"

She continued searching around the room. "Sweetie. Did you lose Bhakti and Samah?"

No response. "Go find them and bring them back. They're too young to be roaming around alone in the wild. Tom is out there waiting to pounce. And there are cobras and hawks and all kinds of enemies of little kittens." I patted her and led her to the door.

Later in the evening, I saw her walking around alone. No kittens. I went behind the building. "Bhakti. Samah. Samah. Bhakti," I called. But no kittens.

Though Sweetie was a wonderful mother, she could be somewhat daffy and a bit forgetful. As I said before, I didn't always trust her judgment. With a heavy heart, I recited my Sanskrit chanting, did my meditation, and went to sleep.

The next morning, no Sweetie. No kittens. Later, in the garden, I came across two young English girls named Toni and Teri. They were looking for frogs in the lotus pond. "Hi. Have you by any chance seen two little kittens?"

"No. Kittens? We love kittens. What are their names? How old are they? Are they lost? Can we help you find them?" The questions poured out in torrents.

Kids are the best kitten detectives! Armed with information and pure motivation, they began their search. "Samah, Bhakti, Bhakti Samah," they chimed with their musical English accents. But to no avail. Bhakti and Samah were nowhere to be seen.

I informed the doorman and the floor monitors to keep their eyes open for the missing kittens. I knew they thought the whole thing was ridiculous, but they agreed to help anyway. In India, cats are not necessarily considered as cherished household pets, so, unfortunately, they may not always be treated with the humaneness and respect all beings deserve.

The following afternoon, one of the volunteers sitting on the third-floor veranda said she'd heard kittens behind the building.

"How long ago?"

"Maybe about an hour ago."

Oh, how I wished these women had told me then! I went behind the building. "Bhakti. Samah. Samah. Bhakti."

My calls went unheeded. It was difficult to explore in this wild and rocky terrain. I passed the tool shed to return home. I turned around to give one last look—there was a big fat mongoose! He had just emerged from around the corner. He stood there in silence and stared at me. From the look on his face, I was afraid he had just eaten a good dinner.

Every cell in my body was filled with dread. The mongoose is the only animal in all of nature who can kill a cobra. Oh no, I thought. If they killed cobras, what would they do to kittens? I had never, ever seen a mongoose before. What was he doing here now in this particular territory? Though I did not give up hope, I began to fear the worst. If he wanted to eat the kittens, it would not be difficult. But maybe he liked them and thought they were cute, so he decided to let them live and go after a more substantial dinner. "Oh God, please protect these little kittens," I prayed. The mongoose stared at me for a long time before he walked away.

When they didn't return by evening, I had a sinking feeling in the pit of my tummy. The mongoose must have eaten them. I began to mourn their premature departure from this planet. And this time there were no "what ifs" because I knew there was nothing that I could have done differently.

# 15

## THE POWER OF MAYA

A day or two passed before Sweetie and the kittens returned. I was ecstatic. They were all welcomed like royalty and were treated accordingly, with the love and respect we all deserve.

It was then that I began to question the illusory nature of my perceptions. My protectiveness and fears for their safety must have caused me to see things that really didn't exist. For example, when Sweetie returned to my room without the kittens and began pacing around, maybe she wasn't really looking for them. Maybe she just felt a bit restless indoors. After all, she wasn't searching behind the trunks or under the shelves, like the time when her babies had been killed. In retrospect I saw how my mind made certain assumptions about a situation based on my preconceived ideas, not on reality. Kitten *maya*[8] was the tiny little universe God used to reveal the larger nature of maya in all situations. The cat guru was helping me see how illusory nature functions. Microcosm is a reflection of macrocosm.

---

8 *Maya* is that aspect of the Goddess within the human psyche that causes us to mistake the unreal for the real. Due to the limited nature of our senses and mind, the ever-changing forms of the universe are viewed as solid entities, separate from one another, existing in and of themselves. Maya can prevent us from experiencing the ongoing wholeness, continuity, and interconnection between all things. As we become more aware of her veiling power, she gradually helps us to realize reality, including the real nature of our own soul.

Now that I was aware of this fact, Mother Nature would test me again and again to help me bring this awareness into practice.

The next day Sweetie took the kittens out to the building across the street, called East Nine. As she and Tom also liked to romp on that roof, it was essential that their children be introduced to their entire territory. This time, I accompanied the explorers on their walk and left them when they crawled under the locked door. Then I just let them be and do their thing.

The next morning as I walked up the stairs of East Nine, I was greeted by a very angry woman—Loretta, the one who had given me the lettuce seeds. It seems that Bhakti and Samah, in a fit of enthusiastic ecstasy, had trampled her vegetables. The newly planted lettuce and tomato saplings had a lot more growing to do before they would be strong enough to withstand the joyous onslaught of Bhakti and Samah! When she tried to shoo them away, they came running back and jumped on the water bucket to drink and scattered her newspapers everywhere, creating a bedlam that was difficult to repair. "All cats and dogs should be neutered," she said. "Give them to someone to adopt who'll keep them inside."

"I can understand your feelings," I said. "I'm really sorry the kittens trampled your vegetables." It was only right that I apologize for their misbehavior, as they could not do so personally. "But this was their first day out in the building alone. They didn't realize what they were doing. I'm sure we can train them or find some way to keep them away from your plants. You can just say 'No!' real loud and scare them away."

She didn't seem open to the tedious prospect of kitten training. As she was involved in a long-term construction project in her room, I had a great idea. "What about building a partition door on the veranda, and I'll pay for it?"

"No. My neighbor won't like it. You'll have to keep the kittens in your room, away from here."

What Loretta didn't realize was that the building had been Sweetie's territory long before she had ever moved in. I proceeded to promise her that I would do my best to keep the kittens away from her territory. As part of the pact, I immediately brought some water and milk to the fifth-floor landing, which became my daily routine, and I explained to Bhakti and Samah that the plants and water bucket on the third floor were absolutely off limits! I knew they understood everything. Training was all just a matter of time—and patience.

When I bumped into Loretta again, she related that the kittens were still trampling her plants.

"Please try to love them," I said. "They are so innocent and sweet. They can learn."

"You should give them away for adoption or keep them indoors," she repeated emphatically.

Her heart was hardened. And little did I know that I was acquiring "enemies."

# 16

## THE FALL

One day when I went to East Nine to bring milk, Samah was sitting there with Sweetie. But Bhakti was nowhere in sight. "Sweetie, where's Bhakti?" I enquired.

No response.

I began to look. "Bhakti. Bhakti."

No meows.

Down the stairs I went, around the street, behind the buildings. "Bhakti. Bhakti."

No Bhakti.

Again the fear returned to the pit of my stomach. "God, please help Bhakti, please bless Bhakti."

I asked the doorman if he had seen her. "No," he said. "Only the mother and the black-and-white one."

"Well, please keep your eyes and ears open. I'm afraid she's lost."

Later in the evening, he said he heard meows coming from the second floor. I went up and looked. I called. No Bhakti. After returning to my building, I too thought I heard faint meows. Was it my imagination? When I tried to trace them to their source, they stopped. That night I went to bed with a heavy heart.

The next day Sweetie and Samah were about, but no Bhakti. Again I walked down the road with open eyes and ears. No Bhakti. Then I tried the building once more. An Australian woman was sitting out on the third-floor veranda. "Did you by any chance see a little gray-and-white striped kitten?"

"Yes I did," she said, to my utter amazement. "She's on the outside of the building near the shaft next to my kitchen, holding on for dear life. She was crying all night but I thought it was a pigeon. Only now do I realize it's a kitten."

She took me inside to her kitchen window. The shaft was a large square drop. On the other side of the cement lattice-work stood Bhakti in a straight vertical position, her sharp claws clutching through the decorative holes in the cement.

"Bhakti. Bhakti. Don't worry. Good girl, Bhakti. We'll rescue you. Good girl, Bhakti."

The tiny kitten stood there, firm in her determination to clutch onto life. What an instinct for self-preservation! I don't know if she recognized me or not. I couldn't imagine the horror of maintaining that fearful position all alone throughout the long cold hours of night, without any milk or water, without the security of the warm cuddly body of her mother—just crying all night.

"Hold on, Bhakti. I'm going to get help. I'll be back."

The Australian lady said, "My daughter's name is Bhakti." She quickly continued, "Try to find a board and maybe we can put it from the kitchen window to the ledge of the shaft. Maybe she'll squeeze through the hole in the cement and walk across. If that doesn't work, get a workman to climb up the pole of the shaft and carry her up to the roof."

I could feel myself getting hysterical inside. I wasn't thinking clearly. My fear seemed to be taking over completely. The mind flashed back to a moment ten years before, when Sai Baba said, "You are hysterical." Yes, he was right.

I looked in the junkyard for a board. The only things there were heavy metal pipes too narrow to chance and impossible to lift. Of course Bhakti was a superb climber and had lots of experience walking on the narrow rim of my desk, but that was qualitatively very different. In my hysteria, I forgot there was a board on the fifth-floor landing of my building. In retrospect, it might have been too short anyway. But my fear interfered with the clarity that might have remembered and given it a try.

I ran around like a person in sleep. First to the man in the mainte-nance office, I explained my dilemma. I guess no one thought of getting a ladder because they didn't have any that high. They gave me the key to the roof and suggested I find a sweeper to climb the pole. None of the sweepers spoke English. I found an interpreter.

Upon scrutinizing the situation, the first sweeper we brought refused. He said he couldn't climb down the pole. The interpreter brought another man who said he could do it. I told him to wait and I would look for a con-tainer where he could put Bhakti. He said he would place her in his cloth and she would be fine. I had lost all sense of judgment. Clearly, Bhakti's safety was not in my hands. I was looking to a sweeper to be the vehicle for saving her life. Yet, deep down, I feared he might be one of those people who did not like cats. "Oh God. Please help Bhakti."

I unlocked the roof. From the square opening on top I could see the shaft and some of the pipe, but I could not at all see Bhakti. The man entered and began climbing down the pipe. On my way down to the third floor, for some strange reason I locked the roof door. As I hurried down, I saw the Australian woman ahead, running down the stairs.

"Bhakti fell," she gasped.

"Oh my God."

I must have gone into slow motion, because by the time I made it down to the road, she was already carrying Bhakti. Blood was dripping from the kitten's nose. Her body was crooked. She looked awful.

"Bhakti jumped and landed on the iron manhole cover on the concrete."

I took Bhakti in my arms, patted her, and kept repeating the mantra *Om Sai Ram.*[9]

"I'm taking her to the vet."

"After she fell, she tried to run to the garden but I caught her. She's in bad shape."

---

9 This specific mantra is believed to evoke the presence and blessings of Sri Sathya Sai Baba. The word "mantra" stems from the root *man*, which means to think, to ponder. A mantra consists of words or syl-lables that are repeated in an attempt to steady the wandering mind, develop concentration, and connect it to higher consciousness. Repetition of mantra can be a potent tool for helping a person cross over the world of illusion.

At that instant Joan walked by. I said, "Bhakti just fell off the third-floor shaft onto iron and cement. I'm taking her to the vet. Want to come?"

I felt so relieved that Joan obliged. We hopped into a three-wheeler with Bhakti wrapped in my shawl. Joan had some holy ash, which I sprinkled all over the poor little kitten. I sang to her all the way, fighting back the tears.

Even the vet looked sad when he saw her. He tested her back and limbs. "The spine is not broken," he said. "She's going to live. I think she's going to be all right."

When he let go, Bhakti tried to jump down from the high table. We caught her on time. Then he gave her a shot for shock, to help her relax and sleep. The assistant, Maria, gave her some milk and Bhakti drank.

"Keep her quiet and indoors for a few days. Apply icepacks to her nose. She'll be all right."

He prescribed antibiotics for infection, allergy and anti-inflammatory pills for the nose and internal injury. In my state of mind, there was no way I could remember what to dissolve in water, what to break in half, and how to measure micromillimeters or use the syringe. I wrote everything down. He wrote everything down. On the way back, Joan stopped at the pharmacy.

"Thank you, God, for saving Bhakti's life," I whispered. Still, I felt very guilty about my hysteria and consequent lack of judgment. Maybe this disaster could have been prevented if my emotions had been less reactive. At least I could have had the presence of mind to find a board before taking such a drastic step as relying on a sweeper to grab her and climb up a pole. I'd much rather serve as a vehicle of Mother Nature with calm, compassionate intelligence and good judgment than be her vehicle of blatant fear and hysteria. But ultimately, we can only be what we are in the moment and hope to learn from our mistakes. There is no blame.

Shortly afterwards, Mother Nature tested me again, and no matter what I did, nothing seemed to work. In the end, all results are fully in the hands of the Great Goddess, in spite of our best efforts—though I firmly believe our sincere efforts can surely influence all possible outcomes, if not in the immediate present, then maybe at some unknown future time.

# 17

## THE SCREAMER

On the way back from the vet with Bhakti in my arms, many obstacles presented themselves. The first was that I had inadvertently locked the door of the roof and completely forgotten about the sweeper who was stuck there. The doorman met me on the road and informed me of my foolish mistake. I gave him the key to let out the sweeper.

Next a teacher stopped me, insisting that we speak immediately about a project I was helping her with. "I'll talk to you later," I said with as much patience as I could muster. This same person had approached me after Bhakti's fall when I was carrying her to the vet.

Then the doorman had some inane questions. "Not now. I'll talk to you later."

Then the lady who sits on the steps[10] came armed with a notebook and pile of questions about me and my room. "Not now. I'll talk to you later."

---

10 Every week hundreds of volunteers from the various regions of India come to engage in service work (*seva*) on the ashram. They serve as helpers in the darshan area, the dining halls, stores, grounds, residences, and offices, as needed. Seva is selfless service, performed as an offering to God, and is an essential part of spiritual training. Every action we perform can be real service if, with conscious awareness, we dedicate our work to the higher, without any egocentric desire for results. In this way, our actions no longer bind our soul and our past karma gradually dissolves, as there is no more fuel to feed it. Self-centered desire serves as the main fuel that continuously perpetuates our karma.

All I wanted was to get Bhakti back to the room safely so she could sleep, and it almost seemed as if some demonic force was trying to prevent that. Finally I made it up the stairs, turned the key to the room, and placed her on the mat. Sweetie arrived immediately with Samah and began welcoming Bhakti with lots of licks and love. The baby drank to her heart's content and tried to go to sleep.

Then Samah started jumping on her. "No Samah." He just wouldn't leave her alone. He wanted to wrestle.

"Samah. Bhakti's hurt. She has to rest. She can't play with you now. Leave her alone and let her sleep." I began to pat Samah.

There was a knock on the door. It was the sweeper.

"I'm very sorry. When Bhakti fell, I completely forgot that I locked the door."

He spoke no English—only rupees. "Fifty rupees. One hour. You give fifty rupees."

Believe me, I had very mixed feelings about this sweeper who had let Bhakti fall. I didn't like the idea of giving him anything for dropping Bhakti. And whatever salary the ashram paid him for sweeping would be paid anyway, whether he was stuck on the roof or not. But it was only right to pay him something for his effort—no matter how unsuccessful. So I gave him thirty rupees.

Meanwhile, Samah was jumping on Bhakti. Sweetie wasn't keeping him away. I closed the kitchen door so Bhakti and Sweetie could be alone.

Samah started screaming and screaming, unbelievably loud, and he wouldn't stop. He only wanted to be with his mother and Bhakti. He too wanted to feed at her breast. I picked him up and started patting him. The only way he would be a little quiet was if I gave him nonstop attention. And this method was far from 100 percent effective. Nothing really helped. He only wanted to be with his mom and Bhakti. "If I let you in, it's okay to drink Sweetie's milk, but do not jump on Bhakti. She needs to rest. Her bones are out of shape. She has to heal."

Samah kept meowing and meowing. He only wanted to be with his family. He probably knew Bhakti was in danger and wanted the reassurance of playing with her. He also might have been a bit jealous that Bhakti was getting all mommy's attention. I patted him again and again. "Calm down, Samah. Bhakti will be okay in a few days. She'll be able to wrestle with you soon."

I gave him a bowl of milk. Clearly, that wasn't what he wanted. His screaming upset Sweetie, and she began jumping on the door to come out. So I opened the door. Sweetie went to him. Soon again he started jumping on Bhakti. Clearly this wouldn't work!

I went to Joan and told her the situation. Although she had no great affinity for cats, she agreed to take Samah so Bhakti could recuperate in peace.

I brought over some milk and carried Samah in my shawl. He never stopped screaming for a second. There was no way this cat was going to shut up. He didn't want milk from a bowl. Only mommy's breast would do.

A few hours later Joan appeared. "Naina. There's no way I can keep Samah. He's constantly screaming. The neighbors are all coming over to find out what's wrong. He stopped crying only for two minutes when a Russian lady who loves animals held him in her lap. You'll have to take him back. I'm sorry."

"Okay, thanks for trying."

As I neared the building Samah's forceful cries could be heard echoing everywhere. What to do? What to do?

"Come on, Samah. We're going home."

"Wha, meow, whaaahhh!" he screamed. People on the road started looking at me strangely.

For several days, until Bhakti was better, my main occupation consisted of being a cat policeman. It didn't work to close the door on Bhakti and Sweetie. It didn't work to lock up Samah. It didn't work to play with Samah and throw his ball. When I tried letting Sweetie and Samah outside, Bhakti wanted to follow. She would cry if they were not all together. After all, this was a family. So I had to be a cat policeman, which wasn't very kind on my nerves but was the best alternative in a truly undesirable situation. We would all get through it somehow.

# 18

## A PILE OF FEATHERS

I t was very difficult to keep Bhakti in for a few days to heal. Whenever mom went out with Samah, Bhakti would cry and get so upset I felt it better to let her go out with them, rather than be agitated and miserable at home. So they all went to the roof of our building together. The sun would be good for Bhakti. I carried her up the stairs, as climbing might still be harmful. Past the fifth-floor landing and under the door they went. Now if Samah jumped on Bhakti, it would be up to Sweetie to set the standards. Maybe he would be less frustrated out of doors, as he would be focusing on the freedom of exploration.

When I told the English children about how Samah kept jumping on Bhakti, Toni said, "He wants to go outside and learn." From the mouths of babes come words of wisdom. No cat who's ready to explore likes being cooped up! There's a big world out there beyond the family. If he had a chance to discover it, maybe he would stop screaming and lose interest in wrestling with his sister.

This child is right on, I thought. When we human beings can find more joyous forms of self-expression that are in tune with our individual readiness and innately dharmic desires, our own unhappiness and aggression also diminishes. Yes, I thought, both in the kitten and in the human being, freedom to develop and mature must be honored. But the point where human psychology departs from kitten psychology is around the issue of liberation.

It is the cat's dharma to develop as part of nature. The cat mother does not teach her kittens anything other than what is natural. It is also the human dharma to unfold as part of nature. But in us, human conditioning and programming often take precedence over nature, superimposed by ego, family, society, country, time, and place. When we can live our own inner essence, in spite of the conditioning of family, time, and place, we too are in touch with our nature—our truly human nature. Then we live in Truth. This Truth remains the same in the past, present, and future. It is valid in east and west, north and south. When we live it, we can make a real contribution to others. *But it takes some effort to leave behind the unnecessary things we have been taught and reach this space of simplicity that comes so naturally to the cat.*

When much of our conditioning and animal aggression have vanished, we begin to experience ourselves as part of one whole, one large family without division, competition, or separation. We become humble and peaceful. Stress dissolves. We know the difference between benevolence and hurtfulness, idealism and greed, truth and hypocrisy. This ongoing conscious process is all part of the human dharma—the prerequisite to liberation.

Bhakti's recuperation was proceeding well. It felt okay letting the kittens go to the roof in the evening, but I didn't want them sleeping out there, as Bhakti still had a long way to go before her healing would be optimal. When I went up to fetch them, Tom was there. He chased Samah to the far end of the roof and jumped on him. Was this play or was it aggression? Was it a wrestling lesson or was it the killing fields? Truly I do not know.

"Come on kittens, let's go home." They did not follow. I picked up Bhakti and Samah and took them home.

In a few minutes Sweetie came to the door. Before I realized what was happening, she entered, proudly carrying something. In her mouth was a dead bird. She dropped it on the floor.

Obviously I didn't have the same appreciation for dead birds that Sweetie had. "Oh no, Sweetie. Take it outside. I don't want a dead bird in my room."

She smiled sweetly and totally ignored my futile plea. Samah took the poor creature in his mouth and began playing catch, dropping it on the floor, twirling it around and around, running to pick it up, throwing it back and forth again and again in sheer excitement. Bhakti didn't want to participate much but watched in fascination.

I could not bring myself to look, while they devoured the poor creature. For I loved birds, as if they were my totem animal. Birds taught me the freedom of flight, the joy of intuition, the love of no boundaries. And they were also my patrons of creation. My first poem ever, written at the age of nine, was an ode to my parakeet Skippy. You can just imagine my disgust as this tiny bird was being relished and devoured beneath my very eyes in the middle of my living room floor!

I opened my eyes to look. All that was left was a pile of feathers.

This is the nature of life and death in the jungle. *All that is left is a pile of feathers.*

Until that moment, I had felt a great affinity with my cat family. Maya made me feel there was no difference between us. Now I knew for certain, there is in fact a great gulf between cat and human. What was wholly good and natural for the cat absolutely repulsed me!

I let Sweetie out. When she returned I checked out her mouth before letting her in. She was holding another bird.

"Sweetie. You stay on the terrace. I'll let Bhakti and Samah come out."

They all ate to their hearts' content. The next morning I moved the metal couch and swept up the feathers.

# 19

## CLIMBING TREES

Bhakti's recuperation continued. I took the kittens down to the second floor to visit Tara. She smiled her broad, beautiful smile, sent them oodles of love, fed them milk, and invited them in to play. They liked her room because it had so many wonderful places to hide—lots of furniture and great cushions to get lost in. Under the bed, behind the long hanging bedspread, it was particularly cozy and private. We chatted while the kittens enjoyed their visit. Then they wanted to go out to play on the veranda, so I let them out.

Samah had a sizable scratch on his nose from the time Tom pounced on him. Now Tom came to the door. Tara was the only one in the building who fed him. Sweetie had many friends because she was so sweet, but no one liked Tom because he was so paranoid and unfriendly. This was the perfect time to observe Tom with the kittens from a safe distance. I wanted to know what was really happening—was it play, or was it murder? I kept my ears open, as well as the door. Before long, I heard a hostile growl. Tom was up on his haunches growling at Bhakti as if he was about to pounce. Clearly this situation was not yet safe.

"Bad boy, Tom. Do not growl at Bhakti. You go."

He ran away. Something had to be done about this cat! What I could not understand was that Bhakti and Samah were fascinated by him, drawn to him, and even loved him in spite of his abusive and murderous tendencies. When they were with Sweetie on the fourth-floor landing and Tom appeared, they always wanted to hang out with him, reach out to him. At first I was scared. But surprisingly enough, they would watch in fascination to see what he would do. After all, even though he was a brute, he was family! More often than not, he would growl at Samah. But that didn't prevent the little kitten from wanting to get close to him. If his growling became too fierce, Samah would run away in time. Even battered children love the parents who beat them. Because children of all species are so close to God, they are simply a reflection of unconditional love, no matter what treatment they receive in return. Of course, Tom was their only male role model. And as their mother was so wonderful, her example also influenced them by reinforcing their loving nature. But that would all too soon be ending. Later, there would be a miraculous turnabout in Tom's behavior. But for now, I had to remain alert.

For the first time ever, I started to take Bhakti and Samah out to the garden. As they were continually being sidetracked by such delectable spots as the dark secret ground under the parked cars or the metal girders in the junkyard, I found it advisable to carry them, so we could make it to the garden before sunset. Later there would be plenty of time to explore. Human time slots do indeed interfere with the natural flow of events!

I placed them on the ground near the lush tropical plants. They looked ecstatic. Soon they stepped on and explored and tasted different leaves and simply enjoyed basking in the sun, in natural surroundings. I felt this was their true territory. Although they loved it, they made no differentiation between this lush paradise and the heaven of the junkyard or the joy of the dust under the cars. *It was all equally good to them. And that's why they were so happy.*

Samah still tried to wrestle with Bhakti, but much less frequently. Sometimes he glanced my way to see if I was looking, before jumping on Bhakti. And he was beginning to respond to "no." Life was beautiful once again. But I had no clue that this peaceful lull between two storms would soon be coming to a close.

The next day as I was returning from bhajans, I saw Sweetie outside with the babies, teaching them to climb the tree in front of our building. "Teaching" is the wrong word. She wasn't exactly teaching, but was allowing them to explore in her presence. Like any proud parent, I was very happy with their new growth and development. Then Joan walked by.

"Look at Bhakti and Samah climbing the tree." She stopped to watch.

Samah climbed up the trunk of the tree and just hung out for awhile. After a little hesitation, he proceeded to climb down. Bhakti climbed up the trunk of the tree and, after a little hesitation, felt afraid to climb down—so where was there to go but up? Bhakti continued climbing up. She had not yet learned that what goes up must also go down. Sweetie did nothing.

"Bhakti. Come on down, Bhakti." She stood there watching us.

"Sweetie, why don't you go up there and show Bhakti how to climb down?"

Sweetie did nothing. Her philosophy of education was "Let the child sink or swim." Nature has absolutely no use for kids who can't make it on their own. Yes, she allows for suckling and imparting hunting skills, but in other things, the kids are on their own. As for me, coming from a race of humans and not cats—at least in this life—I feel children sometimes need human intervention beyond the range of genetic preprogramming and poor parental judgment, when they get into tough situations. Otherwise they could die. But in deference to Sweetie and Mother Nature, I would give Bhakti some time to come down on her own. This was a gross error on my part, since Bhakti remained high up in the tree, as if she were securing her territory.

The trunk was too vertical and thick for me to climb, or else I would have gone up there in a flash, while there was still time to catch her. The doorman wanted to climb up but I did not like his vibes, and the memory of what happened with the sweeper still lingered in my mind. So I sent someone to the maintenance office to get a ladder. He said they had only one, and that it would be available after six. I did not wish to wait that long, so I proceeded to the office on my own.

"Madame. We don't have any ladders," the man said.

"What about that one?" I asked. You can never get a direct answer out of some people.

"You can take it," he said.

A volunteer carried it over to the tree. He seemed very much afraid that I was never going to return the ladder, as he kept asking me my room number and name, and made me promise I would bring it back.

The "ladder" was a homemade bamboo contraption that was missing some rungs, and in some areas was tied together with cloth. By the time we arrived, Bhakti had climbed much higher. In fact, she had really gone out on a limb—a very narrow one at that! I walked up the ladder and called to her. There was a huge gulf between the end of the ladder and Bhakti. And just as she was afraid to go down, I was afraid to go up. I used to love climbing trees when I was in my twenties, but some years have passed since then.

"Bhakti. Come here, Bhakti. Let me help you down." She stood there looking at me and wouldn't budge. Every now and then she tried taking a step or two and stopped. The situation was now getting desperate. Even Sweetie deemed it necessary to alter her philosophy of education!

Finally, Sweetie began climbing the tree to rescue Bhakti. But she was too fat and too heavy to go out on the limb, as it would surely break. So after sizing up the situation, Sweetie opted for survival and soon climbed down. Though Bhakti watched, she didn't seem to learn much about how to climb down, from her mom's example. The kitten remained firmly where she was and would not budge.

Many people going by stopped, inquired, and smiled, but no one came up with any useful suggestions. The volunteers who sit on the third floor near the treetops thought it was all a big joke. As I told you before, some people in India do not regard cats as pets, and may not treat them with the compassion and respect we would like all beings to receive. Joan went to sit on the mattress on the ground floor. It was wet from Samah's pee. Her sari could be washed.

Meanwhile, two hours went by. Soon it would be dark and cold. What to do? Some action was definitely required. But what? Joan said, "Let's pray together."

We sat cross-legged on the ground and prayed to God with all the sincerity, yearning, and good will that lives in our hearts. A couple of minutes later, a kindly Indian man came over and said he wanted to help. He was the new doorman on duty. I liked his vibrations. He said he could climb the tree and rescue Bhakti.

But this man was quite old, with his wholesome wrinkles and whitish-gray hair. I didn't understand how he would be able to climb that far up, at his age. "Don't worry," he said. "I can do it."

He was barefoot. He seemed very loving and secure. "I come from a part of India where we have lots of coconut trees. I climb up very high all the time. Don't worry. I can do it."

Something about his manner inspired great trust. And I had no choice but to trust him. After all, he was sent by God.

Up and up he went, climbing adroitly. This man was an unbelievably skillful climber. As he approached very close to Bhakti, while maintaining his weight on the trunk, he elongated his body, with his arms stretched out on the limb. He was getting closer. One more reach and he seemed to catch Bhakti. I thought she was in the palm of his hand. It was at this very moment that she jumped!

"Oh no," my heart thumped, "a repeat performance!" But at least this time she fell on the soil, as opposed to an iron manhole cover on hard cement. I ran after her and so did Sweetie. Sweetie caught up with her first and began licking her. She took Bhakti under the door into the toolshed, where they remained for some time alone in peace.

I carried Samah home. "Don't worry, Samah. Bhakti's going to be okay." As my voice lacked conviction, it sounded hollow. Joan went home to wash her sari, which by now had fully dried.

# 20

## THE VICTORY OF LOVE

Only about five days had passed between Bhakti's two falls. But miraculously enough, I do not think she was badly hurt by the second fall. Her bones still looked somewhat out of shape, and she did not start playing again for quite some time. But the major effect was undoubtedly psychological. Understandably enough, as we human beings do, Bhakti became fearful.

It was several weeks before I saw her climbing up the mattress outside my room. But in spite of my anxiety, I knew deep down that she was resilient and would surely recuperate. Hopefully, she would also reconnect again with her joyful spirit.

Joan related an encouraging story about her daughter. She began walking at the age of nine months and did quite well. Then she fell, a hard and painful fall. From that moment on, her major form of locomotion returned to crawling. She refused to walk again till she was a year and a half. But once she was ready to try again, she did just fine, almost as if nothing had happened.

"O dear Bhakti, may this happen to you," I thought. Yes, the adventurous spirit gets crushed for a while till our body and judgment mature enough to be able to work in harmony with the different parts of ourselves. This is Mother Nature's built-in way of protecting her children from overall catastrophe. Be it in kitten or human, the guiding principle for maintaining life rests in this law of harmony. When the mind is mature enough to accompany, balance, and support the instincts, life on earth thrives—both individually and collectively. If the instincts are not mature enough to catch up with physical and emotional growth, they can lead to destruction. In the kitten, physical growth is needed, before the instinct to explore can be safely followed. In the human being, the godly instinct of compassion for all beings and for mother earth needs to catch up with the animal instinct of territoriality and its inhuman manifestation of egocentric greed. Egocentric greed, unchecked, leads to the overriding philosophy that money should be the underlying foundation for the entire society. This erroneous belief, in turn, leads to stress, unending desires, and living death.

In contrast, when dharma becomes the basis for individual action, such desires actually end quite naturally. Then economic prosperity can find its rightful place in the life of an individual, without giving way to greed. And the wealth of wisdom will flourish and nourish our daily lives. *For greed rules only as a cheap substitute for love.* Dharma leads to wisdom, which is our greatest natural resource.

As an embodiment of the Goddess, the animal can serve as the spontaneous support, the link, for our inner transformation. Manifest in an animal, the Goddess can help us offset the impatience caused by stress, the violent emphasis of the media, or the alienation and conformity that arise from the idolatry of technology. Through this ongoing example of natural love and uncluttered mind, we can learn to differentiate gold from garbage. Then our conditioning will dissolve and our pain become irrelevant—if, indeed, we are truly motivated to take the next step.

Loving and caring for animals helps all children maintain and feed the natural spark of love inside, which in turn allows our inborn sensitivity to thrive. I say "our" because we are all children of the universal Mother. Each of us has a child inside who needs to be able to live out this innate love spontaneously, unhampered by the falsity of society's mechanistic conditioning and constricting demands. In this way, the inner child can grow up to be a compassionate human being, who appreciates everyone and everything. When we no longer allow ourselves to be ruled by the insensitive ethic that so many adults believe is necessary for "survival" in today's insane, stressed-out world, the inner child can begin to live and thrive and reclaim its primal place in life—bringing openness, spontaneity, and joy to our unnatural and constricted lives. The animal can lead us back to our innate, flowing essence of love—that we might each become truly human and whole.

Just as I finished writing this paragraph, while sitting on a bench in Central Park in New York City, an older Asian woman approached me and began to speak. She was from Japan—Osaka to be exact. We chatted for a while. My heart went out to her. She looked so thin and pale. I wondered if nuclear fallout from the atom bomb had caught up with her. But she seemed happy. With love in her heart, she said, "Central Park like park in Japan. People here very friendly, very nice like Japan."

I sent her love and a smile, clasping my hands together in the Asian greeting, which in India says something like, "The God in me sees the God in you." She clasped her hands and bowed in return.

Something in me sensed she must have had a tough life. Maybe her father was killed by American bombs. But her heart held no bitterness. It was filled with forgiveness and love. She wanted me to know that.

It felt as if the Goddess had sent her at that very moment to reveal something of great importance to human beings:

The loving human heart is the most powerful force on earth. The dominance of the loving human spirit will prevail over all the forces of darkness and materialism. Insensitivity and greed can only lead to destruction when the ego becomes disconnected from the inner loving heart. When we truly care about humanity as a whole, there is no place for selfish interest. It is up to each one of us individually to discover a way of not allowing these inhuman forces to reign victorious and take precedence over our innate sacred heart of love.

The loving heart can surely reign supreme, no matter what—in spite of all the unconscious mechanical, hypocritical forces. But we must each remain aware of the threat, so as to prevent our egoism and conformity from gaining precedence over our innate capacity for the natural expression of our universal love.

This is what kittens and children and dogs and birds and the lady from Osaka have come to teach.

• • •

Sweetie spent lots of time at home with Bhakti and gave her oodles of love and milk and licks, to her heart's content. With awe and reverence, I pay homage to this wonderful teacher, who revealed the art of dharma through her loving example.

# 21

## THE WEANING PROCESS

The unbelievably trying phase of life called the weaning process crept up on us all too soon. The vet had told me to start feeding the kittens milk in a saucer when they were around six weeks old. He thought they would leave the breast behind when they were about two months old. Well, let me tell you, it wasn't that simple!

In the beginning, Bhakti used to sniff Sweetie's dinner of milk or curd and rice and try to eat it, long before she was six weeks old. So when I put the kittens' first saucer down on the floor, Bhakti drank immediately and really liked it. Then Samah took a few licks. He thought it was just okay. But later, when he realized that this cow milk was meant to replace cat milk completely, he began to rebel, for nothing else in the whole wide world could come close to Sweetie's cat milk! He also loved cuddling with mommy. No way was he going to give that up. That's when he began continuously meowing and screaming, and I wanted to change his name from Samah, which means equal-minded, to something more appropriate. But it was too late.

Sweetie and I formed an alliance, which consisted of a bond of nonverbal communication and collusion surrounding this important issue. She taught me everything I know about kitten weaning. First, she'd feed the kittens for a short time, and just as they really got into it, the tease would walk away, cover her chest, and not allow them near. Then it was my turn to step in and bring saucers of milk. Sweetie eyed me with a knowing smile. "Go ahead. Get the milk now," her eyes seemed to say. If the kittens persisted in chasing her, I was to let her outside so they would have no choice but to go for the cow milk.

It all sounds simple enough, but somehow in practice it became very complicated. Sweetie would stand outside near the door, and when she heard Samah screaming, she'd meow to come back in. This cycle proceeded several times, back and forth, back and forth, in and out, in and out, until I really got sick of it. That's what happens when you allow yourself to be controlled by a cat! In a flash, I bowed out of the game.

Then Sweetie started again repeating the in-out behavior at times that had nothing to do with the weaning process—in the middle of the night, for example. Now my patience was really running thin. Sweetie was exhibiting ambivalent behavior to the extreme. Why was it so difficult for her to make up her mind between in and out? Finally I let her stay outside and meow and turned on my white noise machine—waterfalls, babbling brooks, and the like. It really didn't help much. She repeated the same process the next night. And the neighbors didn't even have a white noise machine!

Sweetie was also getting quite fat. Yet the vet thought she couldn't get pregnant again until she stopped nursing the kittens. I hoped with all my heart that he was right, but I had my doubts.

Soon after Bhakti's second fall, the weaning process was interrupted, as were the hunting lessons. Sweetie kept the kittens inside and started feeding Bhakti almost exclusively with her own milk. I assumed this was because mommy thought her own milk would be healthier for the recuperating Bhakti. Soon Samah was ready to go out to the roof on his own while mother and daughter spent some alone time together. But I began to wonder if Sweetie was sick. She seemed so lethargic, sleeping most of the time. Once she vomited. Was the big belly caused by parasites or worms? I asked the vet to come for a home visit, but he never showed up.

Time was passing quickly. The two-month deadline for the completion of the weaning process came and went. Fortunately, I encountered a woman named Padma, who was very experienced in kitten behavior. She informed me that the desired moment could occur anywhere from two months to one year, but that most kittens are weaned by three months. If you recall, weaning was so crucial because Tom would no longer be interested in killing the weaned kittens—at least according to the vet. Then one day when I went to pat Sweetie she hissed. "Sweetie. What's happening?" I asked.

No response. Then she hissed at Bhakti and Samah.

"Sweetie. How could you do that to your babies?" They looked so hurt and shocked. But this cruel hissing would repeat itself many, many times in the not too distant future.

Something highly unusual was happening. She didn't let the kittens near her. They were being forced to drink cow's milk.

The next day Sweetie cuddled up on the kitchen shelf with the pots and pans. She stretched and smiled and purred just as she had done while giving birth two months before.

"Oh no, Sweetie. If you're pregnant again, you're not going to have your kittens in here. Once is enough!"

She understood perfectly and went outside. I guess it must have been frustrating for her too, not being able to go in and out and back and forth with all the ambivalence that came so naturally. The next morning I looked around for her on the veranda. She was nowhere to be seen. But there was the box that I had placed outside in front of my room some time before. I opened the lid. Inside were three tiny infant kittens. Sweetie was feeding them. Two were all black and one was black and white. They looked just like her.

What a fertile cat! She must have conceived only a few days after Bhakti and Samah were born. How beautiful. How adorable. I made some round air holes in the box and brought Sweetie her milk. The cycle of nature continues—right under my nose and without my knowledge. I must be awfully dense!

PLATE 1. *Brand new kittens enter the world.*

PLATE 2.
*Yin and yang.*

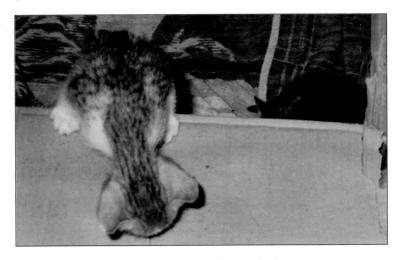

PLATE 3. *Bhakti climbs over the box.*

PLATE 4. *The exploration begins.*

PLATE 5. *Samah ventures into the living room.*

PLATE 6. *Observant awareness.*

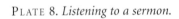

PLATE 7. *Samah and Bhakti pose for a portrait.*

PLATE 8. *Listening to a sermon.*

PLATE 9. *The pocketbook game.*

PLATE 10. *Under the rooftop door!*

PLATE 11. *Havoc at the altar while Baba looks on . . .*

PLATE 12. *The fierce Bhakti.*

PLATE 13. *Now Samah has the upper paw!*

PLATE 14. *Samah screaming after the fall.*

PLATE 15. *First day at the park.*

PLATE 16. *Samah on Tara's terrace.*

# 22

## THE CYCLE CONTINUES

The big covered box outside was now off-limits to Bhakti and Samah. Whenever they went anywhere near it, Sweetie would hiss. So the kittens spent their time on the veranda sitting on the couch, under the couch, or in the plant pots. Whenever Sweetie passed, she would hiss at them. Understandably, they still responded with great hurt and shock each time. Once, when the kittens were on the ground-floor veranda of the opposite building, Sweetie actually went out of her way to cross the street for the express purpose of hissing at Bhakti and Samah. She certainly took her new responsibility very seriously. But this was going a bit too far!

I don't think the kittens understood the rationale for Sweetie's sudden change of heart. Only later would they come to know for sure. It was terrible for them to have a mother who had been so wonderful, loving, playful—almost perfect—suddenly turn against them. My heart ached for them.

"Kittens. It's not that your mommy doesn't love you. She's got new babies now who need her milk more than you do. If she didn't hiss at you, you'd be taking all her milk away from the babies."

They seemed to listen, but I do not know if they really understood.

"Kittens. To be honest with you, personally I feel the babies came much too soon. But your father Tom is a very persistent guy. Now the new babies are here, and you kittens are old enough to drink cow's milk." They eyed me with a neutral stare.

"Bhakti. Samah. I'm sorry you're losing your mommy at such a young age. Everything will work out." They turned and sauntered to the fourth-floor landing.

"Come on, kittens. Let's go to the roof."

Now they were following me as if I were their mom. In the remaining time I had left with them, I would try to be as good a mom as possible.

Bedlam in the room calmed down a bit without Sweetie around meowing and sauntering in and out. Every afternoon I took the kittens to the garden. In the morning, they went to the roof alone or hung out in the opposite building. Once, Bhakti was chased by a big dog, but the doorman intervened in time. He told me always to bring a big stick to the garden, as this dog was after her. As for Samah, he sniffed out dogs and scooted up a tree long before they ever came close enough to be a threat. Until Bhakti recuperated, she would require some watching.

Whereas Samah had been more upset psychologically from letting go of mommy's milk, Bhakti became upset physically. Samah missed the breast so much. At every opportunity, he began sucking Bhakti's chest looking for milk. She simply did not appreciate it one bit! At times I had to intervene to protect her.

Ever since the weaning process began, Bhakti had ongoing diarrhea. Fortunately, she liked curd and rice, which was much better for her than milk. So I tried feeding her only that, but then Samah didn't like it. He liked only milk. And Bhakti would also drink his milk, in spite of the fact that the yogurt-milk combination can be very difficult to digest, even for a healthy stomach. At the time, it was difficult for me to separate the kittens while they ate, so there were some minor logistic problems that had to be worked through. Eventually, I managed to feed one kitten inside and one kitten outside, and I took the food away as soon as they were finished eating. No more nibbling, only full meals.

Allopathic medicine did not help Bhakti's problem, as she vomited up her pills. Homeopathic remedies seemed to make it worse.

Fortunately, at a crucial moment, later on, I chanced upon a Japanese woman who was an expert on Ayurvedic[11] treatment for cats.

One morning several days after the new kittens were born, I opened the big box on the veranda to give Sweetie her milk. And what did I see? One dead kitten, lying in the plastic on the bottom of the box. "Oh no. Not again."

I sent the dead infant love and asked for God's blessings. This one was black with a white belly, like Sweetie. "Did Tom get her too?" I wondered. Did Sweetie move the other two babies and forget about this one? Or did she become ill and die? I hoped she hadn't suffocated from the plastic. No, I thought I remembered seeing blood. This kitten too was murdered. Was it possible that Samah got to her? I doubted it. It must have been Tom.

I prayed for the new kitten on her journey, wrapped her in a plastic bag, and with a heavy heart and tearful eyes, found a decent place in nature to bury her, behind one of the buildings. Then I returned and threw out the box. Before long, Sweetie arrived and began looking for her baby. Now I knew for sure, the kitten didn't die from an illness, as she must have been alive when Sweetie began moving the other members of the litter.

"It happened again, Sweetie. Your baby is dead. She's with God in cat heaven."

Sweetie continued looking for a while. I patted her. And eventually, I think she understood. Her pragmatism wouldn't allow her to waste time crying over the mystery. She had too much important work to do right now. There were two other babies to feed.

---

11 A form of herbal medicine brought to India by the ancient *rishis* (sages), which helps to balance the four elements within the body, thereby promoting healing.

# 23

## GOODBYE, ROOF

In the late afternoon, I would go to the roof with the kittens and just be with them while Samah ran around and Bhakti sat or walked. This spot was beautiful and peaceful, with an open vista of deep blue sky, rocks, trees, and craggy hills. The kittens would explore till they reached the end of the roof, then come and sit down next to me. I would pat them to the accompaniment of bhajans. They would purr. We would share our love in simple communion. Life was wonderful again. Though Bhakti didn't yet play, she was clearly recuperating. A little more time and tender loving care, and she would be fine.

One day as I was sitting on the roof with the kittens, our reverie was abruptly interrupted—not by Tom but by ashram "security." They stomped in as if I were a criminal. It seems someone had reported me to the chief of security for committing the crime of going to the roof. One of the volunteers who loved the kittens had warned me that something like this would happen. But rather than change anything, I had deemed it best to see it through to the end and allow events to unfold.

Since a Russian man had tried to jump off the roof two years before, no one was allowed on the roof. Now here I was, surrounded by rough-looking men who acted as if I were being caught red-handed in an illegal act.

I simply said that the kittens needed a place to go where they would be safe from the cars and dogs on the street, and that it was important for me to go with them to the roof, to protect them. I explained about Bhakti's falls and the father cat's behavior, and told them that Bhakti had not yet recuperated enough to be alone on the roof with Tom around. "Please speak to your supervisor and explain the situation. I'm sure he'll let me keep the key."

The main henchman did not seem at all sympathetic to the plight of the kittens and was evidently not an animal lover. "I have instructions not to leave here without the roof key. You give it to me and come to the office between six-thirty and seven to speak to the security chief."

As the man was firm in his determination to possess the roof key at all costs, I handed it over. I also included the keys to East Nine, which he didn't even know about. This turned out to be a huge mistake. At six-thirty I went to speak to the chief. He wasn't there. I returned in half an hour. He still wasn't there. I considered speaking to him in his room, but felt it would be an imposition.

When I returned the next morning, they said the chief wasn't around but gave me the message: "No. You can't have the key back."

"When can I speak to him?"

"Go to the main gate between 7:00 and 7:30 A.M. He's usually there."

When I went to the main gate at the appointed time, he wasn't there. I returned to the security office. They said, "You just missed him. He's walking down the street."

"Come and point him out to me." So we ran down the street. When finally I caught up with him and introduced myself, the man would not listen to one word I had to say. He just kept repeating, "No, no, no," and tried to walk away. I persisted in my attempt to speak to the chief, but he simply would not listen. This person was using absurd hardened tactics to prevent me from going to the roof with a couple of kittens!

The rules necessary for collective functioning need not override compassion. The two need not be mutually exclusive or at odds with one another. The archetypal conflict between maternal caring behavior and paternal collective rules is surely not insurmountable. Can we not find a way to make room for both?

When we feel compelled to follow externally imposed rules without listening to our hearts, our conscience, our own genuine inner authority, the end results are concentration camps or murders at Kent State, or civilian bombings that are justified as an "acceptable and unavoidable" part of war. It's just a question of degree—the underlying principle is the same. Whether in an ashram, the Los Angeles Police Department, a corporation, or the army, the genuine still small voice within must be given its rightful place. Otherwise, true law can never reign. For when we end up following unjust orders, we cannot help but become perpetrators of insensitivity—which is the root of all evil.

The main characteristic of the *asuric* (demonic) mind is insensitivity. It is insensitivity alone that leads to the destruction of human life—the life in one's own heart as well as actual plant, animal, and human life. *Insensitivity leads to destruction.* The only antidote to insensitivity is feeling pain and experiencing suffering. Then the heart is given an opportunity to open. Without experiencing our own pain, how can we ever experience the pain of others, and consequently come to treat our neighbors as ourselves? Consumerism, fleeting pleasures, and mindlessness can never erase the underlying roots of pain. They can only cover them up for a time and prevent our evolution.

While writing this paragraph near the pond in Central Park, I noticed a dead duck floating with his tail sticking up. Next to his head was a tennis ball. Slowly the dead duck was being pulled by the current toward my bench. I was meant to see and feel and experience exactly how human insensitivity kills life—physical life as well as one's own inner life. I thought how low and aggressive a person must be to kill a poor duck with a tennis ball! Then the water turned the duck around. He was closer, stuck in the algae. I got up to look. It turned out not to be a duck at all, but a yellow tennis ball on top of a piece of bent wood and bark that looked like a duck with his tail sticking up.

The projections of maya will continue to maintain their hold over my mind until I can live in a space of infinite love and acceptance that supports all actions, without judgment—including those of the ashram's chief of security. I will remain unable to go beyond good and evil until I have fully embraced the good in nonjudgmental practice in everyday life.

Only then will the illusory perceptions of maya release her awesome, tenacious grip over my human psyche.

So these extraordinary felines continue to teach me to this very day that I must question my views and perceptions, especially when under the influence of my protective instincts and emotions. In this *Kali Yuga* (the Age of Violence), you can waste a lot of precious energy on righteous indignation—if you haven't yet mastered the art of detachment! And we each have our own individual brand of blind spots.

From another perspective, I've always had difficulty following someone else's rules, especially if they make no sense to me and do not feel right. But when I found myself up against a wall with "No, no, no," I was forced to ask my heart what was really happening. An inner voice responded, "It's time for you to give up the kittens. Care for them, love them as part of God's creation, but be not attached. Soon you must say goodbye."

So another person's seeming insensitivity can serve as a teaching for me. When I cannot make a dent in the other, something inside me needs realignment. At first my reaction is anger. But later, this knowledge of my own lack of inner perfection induces gratitude and love in my heart. When I can focus on what I need to learn, as opposed to the injustice of the situation, something wonderful happens. My heart opens.

*Universal love alone*
*can unite the conflicting*
*archetypes of existence!*

# 24

## REPEAT PERFORMANCE

Parting with the roof keys led to big trouble. The kittens began returning to the roof of the opposite building, as the roof in our building was being repaired. One day, when lunchtime rolled around, I went to the door to call, "Bhakti, Samah, lunch." Samah came racing out, but no Bhakti.

I fed Samah some milk and returned to the door to call, "Bhakti, Bhakti. Time for lunch." Still there was no Bhakti. She hadn't had any liquid for quite some time. The sun was hot and I feared dehydration.

"Samah. Go get Bhakti and bring her out." Samah went in, but he didn't come out. As this was before the Ayurvedic cure for diarrhea chanced our way, Bhakti was in dire need of fluids. I also wondered if she had fallen down the shaft. The only avenue open was to go to the maintenance office and request the key. With a little dread in the pit of my stomach, I marched forward.

"Sorry, madam. We have instructions not to give you the key to the roof. Speak to Mr. So and So."

I spoke to Mr. So and So. "Sorry. The higher-ups are angry at us for giving you the key. Speak to Mr. So and So and So."

Then I spoke to Mr. So and So and So and told him that I was afraid Bhakti could dehydrate lying in the sun, or that she might have fallen down the shaft again. Would you believe that no one seemed to care? Not getting into trouble was more important than being caring. Most of them considered it a big joke!

"Madame. I cannot give you the key to the roof without permission from the ashram secretary."

The ashram secretary was at some function and would not return for half an hour. Meanwhile I prayed for Bhakti's safety. When the secretary returned, he gave me permission to get the key, with a little prodding from his wife.

In anxious anticipation, I opened the door. There was Bhakti, lying next to the shaft in the blazing afternoon sun in a lethargic, semiconscious state. I picked her up, gave her some water, and carried her back to the room. She did not look well. She remained indoors for a while and slept.

Little did I know, the same scene would repeat itself the next day. This was Shivarathri, one of the holiest days of the year—the time when the moon is the smallest, and the forces of Mother Nature are energized to the fullest, to help meditators and devotees experience realization. On this particular morning, unbeknownst to me, Sai Baba materialized a *Shiva lingam*[12] from inside his own body. While this was occurring, I was experiencing a very deep inner meditation. This was a state beyond words that felt to me almost like the creation of the cosmos. For a few hours, the exalted presence of loving consciousness lingered. It seemed so natural, I thought it would last forever. And then, "Bhakti, Samah. Time for lunch."

Samah came out when I called, but no Bhakti. I fed him and sent him back under the roof door to get Bhakti. But again this was to no avail. So I went directly to Mr. So and So and So and asked him for the key. Since he knew the secretary had given me permission yesterday, I thought he would give it to me.

"The plumber has it," he said.

---

12 A phallic or oval-shaped stone of various kinds of material, which signifies regeneration and is used as an object of worship and healing. The lingam is viewed as a symbol of the formless God, which is eternal and indestructible. In India, great yogis are known to materialize objects through the power of mental concentration.

"There's no plumber up there. The door is locked."

"He's on another job. He will not return until six."

"Where is he? I'll go and get the keys from him."

"The plumber's in the town. I don't know where."

The only solution was to break the lock. "Shall I go to the Accommodation Office and ask them to send someone to break the lock, or do you want to do it?"

"No. Ask Mr. So and So."

"Where is he?"

"How would I know?" he replied with hostility.

"I really think the keys are here. Why don't you look again to be sure?" After several avoidance maneuvers, he finally went through the motions of looking.

"No keys."

"What if I asked the ashram secretary for permission to break the lock?"

"Go ahead," he said with indifference.

By now, I wondered where my contact with deeper reality had gone. My loving consciousness somehow seemed to have vanished, swept away by a wave of anxiety and frustration. I hated to approach this person again. He never looked at me, and he seemed to exude such disdain. With utter coldness and confusing words, the secretary proceeded to give me a lecture about what an annoyance I was becoming to everyone. He left not an inch to get a word in edgewise. I knew this man loved dogs, but he did not appear to have even a tiny soft spot in his heart for kittens. Finally I managed to blurt out, "If I don't get the key to the roof, a little kitten could die of dehydration."

"If you want to open the door," he said, "it's your responsibility. I have no objection. But this is the last time."

When I told Mr. So and So and So that the secretary had no objection, he miraculously found the key in the exact spot he had been looking before. "The plumber just returned it," he said.

I opened the door. Bhakti was lying in the same place near the shaft in the blazing sun. She was in a semiconscious state. I wondered if she stayed up there to die because she felt so awful. "Bhakti. We're going home. No more roof for a while." I fed her some water and a little curd. She lapped it up.

The next morning before the kittens could sneak under the door, I covered the space with a mattress. I hated to do it because I suspected this was the major hunting ground for Sweetie. The shaft in East Nine was not covered with mesh screens, as was the shaft in our building. Birds gathered there and could be easily cornered—pigeons, small bats, and maybe even sparrows. The cats would have to adapt and find another aviary hunting ground. I had no choice but to cooperate with nature's overall plan.

# 25

## THE EFFECTS OF GOOD AND EVIL

When the asuric forces gain ascendancy over your life, there are hard times ahead. Another embodiment of the asuric mind— egoism combined with insensitivity—was an old man on the ground floor named Mr. Raj. He never spoke softly, he only yelled. It wasn't primarily because he was hard of hearing. He just wanted to feel important, to be noticed. He would scream at cleaning ladies, servants, *dobies* (people who do the wash), construction workers, and doormen. He would also yell at volunteers and friends. Mr. Raj somehow felt it was his God-given work to mind everyone else's business. Two of my neighbors once said, "He thinks he owns the place." At one time, my repeated requests that he make his radio softer or get headphones were clearly not appreciated.

Though I do not know for certain whether Mr. Raj had a hand in preventing me from keeping the key to the roof, I do know he was directly involved in preventing the vet from coming to my room to see the kittens when they were sick. Mr. Raj told the volunteer doorman that no men were allowed in my room. When I explained that the vet was coming to treat the kittens, who were ill, the doorman related that Mr. Raj told him not to allow the vet in my room. I knocked on his door. There was a woman in his room.

"Mr. Raj. The kittens are sick. The vet has to examine them and give them medicine."

"No visitors are allowed in your room after six."

"The vet is not a visitor. You have someone in your room."

"That's different," he said.

"How is it different?" I asked.

"She's from the ashram. No one off the ashram is allowed."

"What you are doing is not right."

He proceeded to call the security office to report me. In India, among a limited, crude segment of the population, making life tough for a woman is sometimes considered socially acceptable behavior. Here, old men with money are often treated with reverence and respect, no matter how foolish they might be. With Mr. Raj as my adversary, I didn't stand a chance!

The poor vet was feeling very uncomfortable. He suggested I bring the kittens downstairs where he would examine them and give them their pills. I agreed.

Shortly after, a "security" officer arrived. I explained the situation. He smiled to himself and hung around while the vet examined the kittens. Unfortunately, the kittens did not like being examined outside and given medicine in a place that was not their territory. Samah tried to run away. Three people were needed to hold him down. Then Bhakti managed to escape and hide under the stairs behind the mattress. I was getting more aggravated by the minute. Any semblance of detachment I might have had over the ridiculousness of the situation quickly vanished when I saw the unnecessary trouble dished out to the kittens and me, which was all caused by allowing the asuric mind to get away with its insensitive and egotistical forms of expression.

There was still a part of me that had great difficulty accepting the presence of "evil" in the ashram. But the ashram was a miniworld, a microcosm of the larger world out there. People there brought their problems and confusion with them. This was not a reflection on the master, but on the people themselves. For the world of maya contains both positive and negative, and we might not always know the difference between the two! If I wanted to remain near the physical presence of the guru, I would be forced to detach.

No matter where we are, it is a very great thing to learn how to be unaffected by the negativity around us. Sometimes this might seem like an almost impossible feat, as we are living under the sway of maya, not yet in touch with the deepest reality. Being at Prashanti Nilayam, with these simple daily happenings, including the mixture of "good" and "evil," peacefulness and agitation, was offering me the opportunity to be in the presence of the highest, most powerful, most blissful energy, which I hope to come to experience permanently within, always, everywhere—in spite of all the agitation around me. It is this same agitation, experienced in the light of the higher, that can lead us to real inner transformation.

I sometimes remember that Shiva drank the poison of the world without swallowing it. The poison remained in his throat and did not affect him. In this way, Shiva saved the world.[13]

Well, as it turned out, the vet's allopathic medicine did not seem to help very much anyway. Bhakti was terribly thin and unwell. She had experienced so much trauma in her young life. Only three months old, and one thing after another. Yet, from inside, she radiated a meditative and steady look, and seemed even more contented than Samah. Sometimes I would watch her sitting there and, in spite of all her suffering, she seemed in touch with a much larger world than what was apparent. Whereas Samah was restless and externally oriented, Bhakti seemed inner and contented, no matter what. Still, I felt she deserved a break. Would the difficulties never end? What to do?

One day, while we were sitting in line waiting to enter the mandir, an ashram resident named Lilo asked, "What's that scratch on your forehead?"

"It's from my kitten. Bhakti scratched when I was trying to give her some medicine."

"What's wrong with her?"

I proceeded to enumerate Bhakti's many ailments, from a scratch on her nose that never seemed to heal due to Samah's incessant wrestling, to the consequences of the fall, to the diarrhea, which was now getting out of control. "Ayurvedic medicine is very good for cats," she said. "I make

---

13 In this story from the *Puranas*, Shiva's neck turned blue from drinking the poison and he was given the name Neelakantha, which means "blue-necked." This aspect of the myth reveals Shiva as the prototype of sacrifice.

my own pills. It always works for diarrhea. Many sick cats are helped by Ayurvedic medicine. I will help Bhakti."

Lilo is the best animal healer I have ever met—so caring and efficient. I had seen several good vets in New York when my wondrous cat Neffy became ill, but that was before I knew anything about the efficacy of Ayurvedic treatment for animals. Lilo combines *pranic*[14] healing and love with her medicinal treatment. She showed me how to make medicine from an Ayurvedic powder called *dadimastaka churnam*,[15] psyllium husk, and honey. The pills can be made beforehand, and stored for a day or two. Here is the recipe:

Combine the powder with a drop of honey and create some tiny pills, just the right bite-size for kittens. Keep until needed. Before administering the pills, place a few drops of water in the psyllium and make a pancake-like dough that will serve as a wrap around the pill. (Psyllium by itself in fluids is a mild cure for many stomach problems.) Then cover with honey to keep the pill soft. Now for the cleansing process:

First wash your hands. Next, sweep your hands slightly above the animal from the top of the head to the very bottom of the body or tail. If you need to hold the animal with one hand, that's fine, but do not touch the animal with the hand that is doing the sweeping. According to pranic healing theory, the practitioner should not touch the patient, as this technique is primarily a cleansing process, rather than a means of transferring energy from one person to another. After each sweep, close your hand, then open it swiftly while making the motion of throwing the diseased energy away into an imaginary fire. Repeat several times. This sweeping process is said to cleanse the etheric body.[16] Next, wash your hands. Now for the hard part:

---

14 From *prana*, the subtle life energy existing everywhere. Within the body, prana manifests as five vital airs present in the breath, circulation, digestion, elimination, and the power of thought. Pranic healing works to cleanse the unhealthy energies from the subtle body and the aura, thereby leading to the healing of the physical body.

15 This medicine is made from eight natural ingredients. The primary ingredient is pomegranate powder, which can be purchased from any Ayurvedic pharmacy. Use one-quarter teaspoon per pill for adult cats and half that amount for kittens. Administer twice a day, morning and evening, on an empty stomach.

16 This aspect of the subtle body is composed of vibrations of vital energy called prana. Most diseases occur first in the etheric body before manifesting in the physical body. The sweeping process helps the body dispel the diseased energy, remove blockages from the energy centers, or *chakras*, and absorb fresh prana, thereby healing itself.

Open the kitten's mouth. Before administering the pill, coat his/her throat with a small teaspoonful of honey and water, to ensure that the pill will glide down easily. Then, to prevent the animal from spitting up the pill, offer some dry cat food that has been soaked in water.

When Lilo did it, it looked so easy. Whenever I tried, several pills were spit up, and extras were required. A couple more lessons were needed before I learned the knack. As Bhakti never wanted to cooperate, I had to wrap her up with a towel to prevent her from gouging my eyes out. She fought medication like a real wild cat!

Samah was different. He usually tried to make pill taking as easy as possible. At times, I thought he was even trying to help me. Though Bhakti fought taking pills tooth and nail, somehow they managed to get down, and within a few days she was much better. One week later, the long-term diarrhea had completely vanished.

What a huge difference between the positive effect produced by Lilo's caring actions and the aggravating effect produced by Mr. Raj's egotistical actions. One way leads to healing, the other to trouble! *Caring and good will versus egotism and anger is the simple difference between good and evil in action.* I felt very grateful to God for sending Lilo to help Bhakti. And I would continue using Ayurvedic treatment for healing Bhakti's nose.

# 26

## A NEW APPROACH

The time was drawing near for me to say good-bye to the ashram. Rumors were afloat that Sai Baba would soon leave for his school in Whitefield near Bangalore. I did not want to go until Bhakti was in better shape. Though her stomach problems had gone away, she still didn't play, and the skin problem on her nose was getting worse. She needed to regain her strength and survival skills before losing her second mother.

Fortunately Tara loved the kittens and would take over the feeding. But she would not be able to invite them in for long, as her husband had asthma. And she would not be able to chase after them if they were lost. Since they were older now, this was the perfect opportunity for transition to independence. However, my major concern remained their capacity to survive. Sweetie had never completed the process of teaching them how to hunt, as she had new babies when they were only two months old. I wondered, "Is it necessary for a mother to teach a kitten where to find a bird and how to kill and eat it? Or is this an instinct so well implanted in the brain that it will just happen when the time was right?" "Experts" offered contrasting points of view on this topic.

I did notice that Bhakti and Samah both loved chasing bugs without ever being taught. On some occasions, they would also eat them. But catching and killing a bird was far more complicated than catching a poor slow bug.

One day when I took the kittens to visit Tara, Tom arrived. Somehow it occurred to me that since they had lost their mother, maybe Tom could learn to be a father. Being a father surely isn't just a matter of procreation, but of ongoing participation in life. Maybe he could teach them how to hunt. "It's time to befriend this murderer," I thought. For I knew deep down that everyone needs love—especially a killer. Maybe if I began to send him love, he would change his ways.

"Hi, Tom." I sent him love. To my utter amazement, instead of running away, Tom actually looked at me for the first time in his life and made that smiling blink of the eyes, so typical of cats, which says, "I send you love back."

Was it really possible? Or was I just imagining it?

"Tom. You know Bhakti and Samah have lost their mother. Sweetie never finished teaching them how to hunt. It's up to you now, Tom. Teach the kittens how to hunt. After all, they are your children."

He just sat there. At least he didn't run away. Whether he understood or not, I do not know. Nonetheless, maybe I was planting seeds, giving him some good ideas for the future. Again I sent him love and told Tara my new approach with Tom. She laughed and thought it was ridiculous. But I persisted in being loving and friendly to Tom. And he began spending more and more time on Tara's veranda.

Soon Sai Baba left for Whitefield. Within two days, thousands of people cleared out. The ashram was wonderfully silent, with no Mr. Raj to contend with. Puttaparthi became a village again, almost like the place I had known ten years before. But Bhakti was still not well. Though "foreigners" were not welcome on the ashram after Baba departed, I would try my best to stay around for about two more weeks till Bhakti was stronger.

For Bhakti was now going to be on her own. Though she might never be a fully wild cat, she would have to learn to defend herself. After her second fall, I tried teaching her how to climb down the vertical mattress on the veranda. I held her and placed one foot behind the other. She got the knack and climbed down again on her own. This was a skill she was learning. But there is a decided difference between a mattress and a tree.

I continued giving Bhakti the Ayurvedic pills for her nose. They seemed to help somewhat, but not a lot. Every day, she was getting a little stronger. She enjoyed the garden and was slowly regaining her cat spirit. One wonderful afternoon, Bhakti caught a big bug. From the distance, I could not tell if it was a scorpion, though it seemed to have a tail. Rightly or wrongly, I assumed it was not. She began playing with the bug. Samah ran over and tried to take it away.

"Samah. No. That's Bhakti's bug. No, Samah. You get your own."

He understood perfectly and went his merry way, as if he had never even tried to steal the bug. Meanwhile, Bhakti dragged the poor creature here and there. Though I don't know if she finally ate him, at least she was regaining her spirited survival skills.

On another occasion in the garden, I saw Samah make a dash for the junkyard across the street. This cat could really run. Swiftly, he climbed up some metal girders and stood on top of them, just watching. A minute later, three wild dogs dashed through the garden. Fortunately, I saw them coming. "Bhakti. Bhakti. Where are you?"

Just in time, she climbed up the cement wall that covered the drainpipe. It wasn't very high, but was just high enough. The dogs stood and barked at her. Unfortunately, I didn't have a stick. As they were wild, they did not understand "Go," no matter how forcefully it was exclaimed. Only when they felt like it, did they finally leave.

One day, I was overjoyed to see Bhakti climbing a tree. It had been many weeks since she had dared try again. And now, she was sensible enough not to go up so high. She seemed to pace herself, and practiced exactly what she could handle. With skill and caution, she climbed down. "Good girl, Bhakti." I felt very relieved. She was learning. She would be okay.

I began leaving the kittens alone in the garden for longer periods of time. Samah would climb and stay high in the tree till after dark, while Bhakti often returned on her own to sit in the sun on the veranda of East Nine. The kittens still did not come back by themselves to eat, but would wait until I called them. Before I left for Bangalore, they would have to learn.

# 27

## PREPARATION FOR SEPARATION

Before long, the transitional training period had begun. The kittens must gradually learn that their new home would be on the second-floor verandah in front of Tara's room. I brought down their mats and their chair. A porter carried down my plants. The couch would go later, as sometimes they still slept there outside. But usually they spent the night in the kitchen or behind the living room curtain.

Tom quickly took possession of the green mat and left the blue-and-white one for Bhakti and Samah. I gave Tara what little dry cat food I had left, and tried very diligently to find more. This turned out to be almost impossible in India. We had been waiting several weeks for some to arrive at Glenand's Pet Shop in Bangalore, but to no avail. It was imported from France to Bombay and for some reason it never showed up. So we had to economize.

Lilo had given me a handful of dog biscuits to mix with the pellets of cat food and soak in water, so they would get soft and expand. The longer they soaked, the wider they expanded. I do not know how the law of conservation of matter and energy worked in this instance, but their hunger was unquestionably satisfied by the larger food pellets. And this prized possession of dry cat food would have to last for quite a long time.

By now, Samah also liked curd and rice, so milk was all but eliminated from their diet, as every time Bhakti drank milk, no matter how diluted, her stomach problems would return. The kittens really enjoyed eating Tara's curd and rice, which was absolutely delicious, so they adapted well to the new transition. I thought it best to tell them what was going to happen—as if they didn't yet know! They surely noticed that I was packing and putting things in the kitchen storage space, where they would remain till my next visit.

When the moment was right I said, "Kittens. I love you very much. But I can't stay here with you. I'm going to leave soon. So many people have gone. I have to go too."

I patted them and felt very sad. These kittens were no dopes. They must have understood—if not my words, certainly the nonverbal feelings I communicated.

"I love you very much, kittens. But I have to go. You're going to have a new mommy now." A salty tear trickled down my left cheek.

They looked at each other. I patted them and tucked them into bed behind the closet curtain.

Communicating with the kittens about the future course of events helped prepare me for the separation as much as it did them. I really needed the transition time, when my psyche would acclimate itself to the loss so I could let go. I had to experience fully the sadness of the loss, before I could separate. How difficult it must be for parents to let go of their children, when they go away to college, for example. But Bhakti and Samah were hardly college age. In human terms, they must have been about six or seven. They were still so tiny and vulnerable. *In order to fully let go, I needed the total faith that God would take care of them.*

In spite of Bhakti's many difficulties, I often felt the hand of God and Goddess supporting her. I needed to know without a doubt that this love would continue supporting and nurturing them both, no matter what. Cultivating faith in a higher presence operating through the material world greatly helps us to let go of fear and attachment. And one prerequisite for faith is openness. It is a myth that faith should be unquestioning and automatic. Intelligent doubt and genuine openness to questioning and reflection can create conditions that allow the universe to respond to our heartfelt inner enquiries. This leads to experience. And experience alone can bring us lasting faith.

People often asked if I planned to take the kittens when I returned to New York. This was out of the question. The idea had never even occurred to me. For these kittens belonged in the ashram. They were born here. This was their home. Their nature was semiwild. Surely, it wouldn't be right to remove them from their native environment within the orb of Sai Baba's presence, where they were born to live out their cat karma.

The animals born on the ashram are quite special and very blessed. And the kittens born there who somehow manage to live are totally blessed. If you recall, Tara had said that only about two or three of Sweetie's kittens had survived, in all the years she'd been having litters. That's an unbelievably poor batting average. And about a month after the birth of Bhakti and Samah, five adorable kittens were born in Padma's home. Two months later they were all dead. Dogs killed three of them, one died of cat flu, and one disappeared. Their premature deaths do not mean that God didn't bless these kittens. It's just that God rarely interferes with the automatic, mechanical functioning of nature. Rather, the divine totality leaves it to human beings to help support the lives of animals and plants. Even when we are well-meaning and loving, we cannot expect to be able to combat all the aggressive, mechanical forces of nature, which are very very potent. Padma was devastated. And she was both loving and knowledgeable.

For her, the realignment necessary was, "Don't get involved. Let them be wild on their own. Let nature take its course."

For me, I believe that one reason the Great Goddess allowed Bhakti and Samah to live was to help me complete my maternal karma in as quick and unbinding a way as possible. Whatever inner yearning to be a mother still lingered unknown in seed form, in the secret recesses of my soul, needed to be lived out as swiftly and as painlessly as possible. For to die with an unfulfilled desire calls us back to earth for a new birth, life after life after life. And I felt that I was not meant to be reborn for the purpose of being part of nature's automatic, mechanical plan. If my destiny were to include another incarnation—O may it serve some higher purpose!

The fewer desires we have, the more evolved we are, the better our chances are for leading a spiritual life, which can truly guide us to ongoing peace and contentment. As you well know, leading a spiritual life does not mean going to church or worshipping some God in heaven, or meditating, while continuing to behave in a mechanical and inhuman way. Rather, spirituality entails being sensitive and caring, with some humble awareness of our own imperfections, alongside the knowledge of how to use the tools that will help us transform our animal nature into our loving human nature, into our universal, Godlike nature. And Bhakti and Samah were helping me on my journey.

# 28

## THE FUTILITY OF PLANNING

I made plans to leave for Bangalore the following week, on Tuesday morning. But Mother Nature keeps teaching me over and over again, "Do not plan." I've learned it's fine to have a more or less general idea in mind regarding what needs to be done. Then allow events to unfold and inform us when the moment is right. This is very different from procrastination. In this way, we establish a partnership with events and serve as a vehicle of harmony. When the mind plans, we tend to impose mental will on the inherent harmony of events, which leads to stress and disharmony, in ourselves and in others. Of course, in Western society, it is essential to plan somewhat. But in India, we come to know for certain that even simple events and outcomes are not in our hands.

I had long since given up the idea of painting and plastering my room before leaving, as this would have meant extra trauma for the kittens. I wanted my last days with them to be peaceful and loving. And they were—sort of.

Unexpectedly, Tara informed me she had to go to Bangalore and would return by Tuesday evening. There was no way I was going to leave without being sure the kittens' new mommy was back for sure. So I canceled my taxi and made a tentative arrangement for Wednesday. I decided to continue feeding the kittens on Tara's second-floor veranda during her absence. Wednesday came rolling around, but she did not return. So I postponed the taxi until the following day.

On Thursday morning I discovered that Tara had returned late Wednesday night. Then she informed me she would be leaving again for a week in May. Immediately I canceled the taxi and began the arduous search for a responsible person to feed the kittens. But who could that be? Most people had already gone. The ashram was empty.

By word of mouth, I tracked down an Italian woman named Jyoti who lived in the village and had a nice yard where her six cats lived. But unfortunately, she would be away that week. Then I discovered an Australian nurse at the ashram hospital. She looked so tired and overworked, there was no way I could impose on her the responsibility of feeding the kittens twice a day. Then, there was someone in town who loved animals, but it turned out she had a dog. Every lead seemed to lead nowhere.

While returning home feeling utterly exhausted and depleted, I happened to notice the gardener. He might not be that "responsible" according to Western standards, but he really liked the kittens. He always kept an eye open for them when they were in the garden, and made sure to shoo away the dogs. Whenever he gave Bhakti and Samah water with the hose, he was careful not to sprinkle them, as they were not fond of baths. He knew when either of them had a cold, without my telling him. And he especially admired Samah's handsome markings, which elicited a huge grin of admiration and appreciation for his beauty. Yes. The gardener was the perfect person to feed the kittens. He would undoubtedly be not only willing but also honored!

The gardener's English left something to be desired, but it was far better than my nonexistent Telugu. "You feed kittens for one week. Mrs. T. on second floor going away. You feed?"

"Yes, yes," he smiled. He already knew I was leaving, as I had asked him to watch the kittens when I left and bring them back to the second floor to eat, if they didn't go on their own.

"No milk. Only curd. Okay?"

"Okay."

"You go speak to Mrs. T. She will explain in Telugu."

"Okay. I go tomorrow before twelve."

Although he didn't show up then, I knew he would come some other time. So I arranged for the taxi to come the following day. As things turned out, the plan was still a bit premature.

The last afternoon in the garden was filled with a very sweet sadness. The kittens and I had been through a lot together. They'd both come a long way in accordance with Mother Nature's plan. Samah was very adept at climbing trees and running and exploring. He was really in his element outside—not too wild, yet not really tame—somewhere in between. His nature was so unbelievably loving. He really listened and understood and tried to please. He would trail after me when I walked very far out of his territory, without a trace of fear. Though much maneuvering was required before I could escape without his getting lost, I had no fear whatsoever regarding Samah. With God's blessings, he would take care of himself and grow up to be a handsome, healthy, and loving cat.

Bhakti too enjoyed being outside. But she was still so vulnerable. Her fall had arrested her wild development and kitten skills. But from another perspective, she became so inner, so deep and peaceful, that it almost seemed as if she had separated from her body. Bhakti seemed like a real yogi. Yogis too could survive, though their aim went far beyond mere "survival." Bhakti served as the perfect example of how events could alter the course of a life, for better or worse. What seemed "worse" in the ordinary everyday sense of activities and survival skills seemed miraculous from another perspective. For Bhakti's capacity for contentment and transcendence always seemed to predominate. Whereas Samah was normally moody and cranky sometimes, Bhakti was very steady in her ongoing happiness. This inner state is difficult to achieve even for the most diligent yogi. And Bhakti was but a four-month-old kitten.

Now, if you believe my notion of Bhakti is romanticized and sentimental, you are absolutely correct. But it is also truthful.

I wanted so much for the kittens to live and thrive, but I knew their fate was not in my hands. I had already done my part and played it as best I could. And soon the curtain would be falling on this particular act, only to rise again for the second act and a new stage of life for each of us.

# 29

## SURPRISES NEVER CEASE

In a state of peaceful reverie, I walked home from my last day in the garden. Samah and Bhakti followed. Then from the second-floor veranda, Tara's insistent voice streamed forth, "Come here quickly! Quick, quick!"

I did not stop to ask what was wrong but zoomed up the stairs. The kittens followed.

"Look," she said as she walked toward the railing of the veranda. At that very instant a tiny black kitten jumped or fell from the second floor to the ground below.

Sweetie started running around in circles. I dashed to pick her up to take her down to the kitten. For the first time in her life, she wouldn't let me hold her. "Come on Sweetie. Hurry up. Let's go down." She looked dazed.

When I got to the bottom of the stairs, Samah was in front of me running toward the kitten. She couldn't have been larger than a tiny ball. I tried to beat Samah to the baby, but he was too quick for me. He looked as if he was about to pounce. He must have thought she was free game for hunting. "No, Samah. No, Samah. No No No!" I boomed.

Miraculously enough, he stopped. He did not pounce. His human understanding and training actually took precedence over his wild instincts. "Good boy, Samah." If a kitten could go against his preprogrammed unruly instinct as a result of loving training, imagine what could be possible for human children! And Samah was only four months old. "Good boy, Samah."

By now, Sweetie had shed her hysteria. She ran over to the little black kitten and started licking her. In a flash, the two of them crawled under the door of the same shed where Sweetie had taken Bhakti after her fall from the tree. I felt somewhat uneasy, but since the infant was walking and Sweetie seemed confident in her instinctive healing capacity, it felt okay to leave her care completely up to the mother. But at that point, I had little choice in the matter. So I returned to the second floor veranda and allowed events to unfold. Bhakti and Samah followed. Behind the plant pot was another furry black ball.

"Sweetie brought them here while you were in the park—two little black ones like Lucifer." Lucifer was one of the kittens who had survived three years ago, and since then had become completely wild.

The new arrivals were totally precious. But what did all this mean for Bhakti and Samah? Imagine the trauma of losing a cat mother, having her hiss at you, then loving a human mother who's going to leave, then adapting to a new home. And to top it all off, your mother moves into your new place with two other baby kittens. What a horror story for Bhakti and Samah! They did not yet fully understand what was going on. I would have to cancel my taxi for tomorrow and observe the situation. It was really important that I leave only when the time felt right.

I took their couch down to Tara's. At least they could have some territory of their own. I hoped Tom would not steal it for himself.

Sweetie was already back with her new baby. Miraculously enough, the little black furry ball looked fine. The two babies wiggled around the plant pots. They were absolutely adorable. But Bhakti and Samah did not think so.

For the first time in her life, I heard Bhakti hiss. She hissed at the baby kittens. She hissed at her mother. She hissed and hissed and hissed. At least she was getting out her anger in a supportive environment and not suppressing it, as we humans tend to do. I sent her love.

Samah just stood there watching. He was on the alert. Would he try to pounce again? No. He just eyed the situation with hurt and disbelief written all over his face. The worst was yet to come. Sweetie started feeding the babies right in front of Bhakti and Samah. Nothing like rubbing salt on open wound! Bhakti hissed again. Now Samah joined in. The two poor kittens just stood there watching, filled with rage, envy, and disbelief. How could their mommy, who had been so good and loving, do this to them?

I suspect Sweetie wanted them to know exactly what was happening. What a climax to our wonderful plans for Bhakti and Samah in their new home! But no matter how difficult, they would have to adapt.

I hung around for a couple more days to witness the adaptation. It turned out to be Sweetie, not Tom, who invaded the kittens' couch territory. After all, it had been hers for quite a while before Bhakti and Samah ever even entered the world. The new babies preferred hanging out behind the plant pots to the left of the door with Sweetie, while Tom's mat was across from the couch. Bhakti and Samah sat on their chair and had to eat inside Tara's room, or Sweetie and Tom would devour their food. But what about Tara's husband's asthma? With God's help, a solution to this difficult situation would evolve in a way that would be equally beneficial for all.

By now, I truly felt it was time to go. I could not keep hanging around till the next crisis. There seemed to be no end to this circle of maya. *Round and round and round it goes in continuous cycle, like a merry-go-round that never seems to stop.* This particular game was no longer my problem. I could now jump off this specific carousel—when the time was right.

Again I sent love to Tom and reminded him that Bhakti and Samah were his children. "Please be good to them and teach them how to hunt. They love you. Love them too." For the second time in his life, Tom looked at me with a smile.

Since the new babies were born, Sweetie didn't like me patting her, but that didn't stop her from coming to my room for milk and then making a swift exit. "Bye, Sweetie. You're a wonderful mom. See you."

I sent love to the two little Lucifer Juniors. So many good-byes already had been said to Bhakti and Samah. I was now sitting with them on my lap on the couch, patting and patting and patting them, trying very hard to hold back the tears. Such sadness swelled in my heart, for having to leave these beautiful youngsters, still so tiny. The doorman walked up to the second floor.

"Madame, your taxi has arrived."

For some reason, the timing was never right for me to show Tara how to administer the Ayurvedic pills. She would treat Bhakti's nose with gentian violet. I would try to get dry cat food in Bangalore and send it to her. And I would see her in Whitefield when she arrived in May. I gave Tara a tearful hug. This new extended cat family was quite a responsibility. What a wonderful blessing she is and ever continues to be for this marvelous family!

I gave Tara another big hug and went upstairs for my luggage. The porters were already there. Bhakti and Samah were following right under my feet, as always. They followed me up. They followed me down. Then they stood on the ground-floor veranda and watched as I opened the door and got into the taxi. I rolled down the tinted window so they would see me in the car and know I was leaving. I did not want them to keep looking for me. They needed to see me go.

They stood still as two statues. My sadness mingled with their sadness. I sent them love. As the car pulled away, instead of waving, I placed my two palms together in the traditional Indian greeting, which says, "The God in me sees the God in you." And that was that. They continued standing there in utter silent stillness, just watching as the car pulled away. As for me, I cried.

# 30

## THE FOUNDATIONS OF LIFE

It was good being in Whitefield. It was good having a room to myself, without kittens jumping all over me whenever I sat to meditate. It was good regaining another degree of freedom, where I would no longer feel directly responsible for human intervention in the traumas of kitten rearing. And yet . . .

There was no real demarcation of lifestyle anymore from one way of being to another. The experience of ongoing living existence was gaining continuity over any specific activity. The sense of being that exists always, no matter what, was beginning to permeate whatever actions occurred in the outside world. No matter what I did, there was some link with the underlying unity of life. *The ever-present invisible support of all actions was becoming more major than the action itself. Maya was loosening her grip over the psyche.*

For me, reaching this point could only have occurred through active participation in the simple, caring difficulties of everyday life. Meditation in a cave alone could never have accomplished what living with kittens did for me. No longer would I separate and segment the sacred from the mundane, the holy from the unholy, the spiritual from the nonspiritual. Whatever we are given in this life is perfect—perfect for our development. How kind of Mother Nature to send us the exact circumstances we need in order to evolve, that we might ultimately shed her dominion over our innate being, which exists always, forever and ever.

The Dutch woman who had organized the Animal Rescue Center in the village of Puttaparthi, where I found the vet, had also opened up a new branch in Whitefield. In such a poor country as India, what never ceases to amaze me is that medical care is often absolutely free. No one pays to bring an animal to the vet. The foundation pays the vet's salary, pays for the space, and unsalaried volunteers work for the clinic. They do it out of love. Their money comes strictly from donation. This donation is also given out of love and not with the motivation of getting a tax deduction.

Poor villagers would bring in their donkeys or stray dogs and never have to pay one cent. This same principle also operates for human medical care. In Sai Baba's hospital in Puttaparthi, the most beautiful architectural aesthetic is coupled with high-tech efficiency and loving medical care. Top-notch surgeons operate at no charge, on poor and rich alike. These institutions thrive through donation and dedication. Hospitals in the U.S., which are undergoing a severe medical crisis with spiraling costs and uncaring ineptness, would do well to ask, "How is it possible in India? What changes are required within the human psyche to make it all possible here?"

In my humble opinion, a totally new way of thinking is required. For this to occur, greed must take a backseat and allow human compassion to emerge. When economics rules the psyche, the spirit of humanity withers. Innate caring intelligence is lost. When this is lost, we are no longer human.

One day after darshan, I saw a tiny baby kitten with gray and white stripes. He looked about five or six weeks old. No mother cat was around. Members of a large Indian family were picking him up and tossing him back and forth from one person to another, while trying to take video pictures of him with their baby. In utter helplessness, he kept squeaking. He was still too young to meow. Finally they put him down. My heart went out to this little kitten. But I knew my days of being a foster mother had ended.

Then a seven-year-old boy named Jack appeared. Jack loved Bhakti and Samah. He told me he had seen the little kitten before, behind a big rock. He too did not see the mother. We waited around a bit. No mom. Soon Jack left to get some milk.

When I returned some time later, the kitten was lapping up her milk. Monkeys nearby jumped from tree to tree. They did not bother the kitten. Across the narrow path, baby puppies suckled at their mother's breast. They did not bother the kitten. He looked absolutely at home here in this high-risk situation. Nearby was an open sewer filled with garbage. What if he drank this water?

Jack picked up the kitten. He squeaked and climbed on his shoulder. "Get him off. He tickles," laughed Jack.

I picked up the kitten. I patted him. I sent him love. As he crawled up my sari, suddenly he stopped, right around the heart chakra. He tipped back his head and looked me straight in the eye. So much love emerged from this little kitten. He just stood there looking at me. I saw all existence in his eyes. I patted him. Jack said he was crying. I had never seen a kitten cry.

The infant's eyes were deep as the creation of the world. They seemed to say what couldn't possibly be put into words. But I knew he had also seen in me what some cats were sensitive enough to perceive. And I acknowledged the same in him. In loving gratitude, I patted him again. Then he crawled up my sari and aimed for the shoulder. His nails got caught in the silk. I knew only too well that baby kittens are born with lethal nails! "Hang around a bit, Jack. Keep your eyes open for his Mom. I have to go."

Neither Jack nor I ever saw this kitten again. Since he was so beautiful, I suspect he was adopted. And in case I had forgotten, this precious, deep little kitten let me know for sure that the concrete personal dimension of love is as essential as its underlying universal essence. Universal love is to be expressed through individuals. Nonetheless, I still harbor the wonderful prejudice that it's much easier and sweeter to have a relationship with animals than with people. Fewer mental variables and no expectations make loving an animal as natural as breathing. Yet in all fairness to human beings, I must admit I've been fortunate enough to meet a few who have totally redeemed the human species.

When the energy of love streams forth freely from the human heart—without divisive selectivity or self-centeredness or smothering attachment—we come to see there is truly a place for us all. And creation can continue.

# 31

## A RAINBOW ENDING

The time for Tara's visit was upon us. I thought back to when I had called her, the day after my arrival in Bangalore two months earlier. She had said she knew I would call. At the time, she assured me the kittens were doing just fine. After my taxi had pulled away, Bhakti and Samah had spent the day hanging out near my room. The volunteer brought them down to the second-floor veranda for lunch. So far so good. The next night I called again. But it was impossible to get through. Though Indian telephones leave much to be desired, I somehow knew that this was a message not to call again. I missed them so much, but now I was to put my attention elsewhere. Finally, two months later, I would hear it all firsthand.

Those of you who have cats know that the only thing one can ever expect from a cat is the unexpected! Will wonders never cease? Tom was now a real father! Instead of growling at Bhakti, he let her play with his tail the way Sweetie used to do. Of course, knowing Tom, he might have been waiting for the precious moment several months down the line when Bhakti would go into heat, and he would initiate her into the joys of sex. I wouldn't put it past him. But for now, I put the idea out of my mind and was delighted that Bhakti finally had a father.

I gathered that Tom was also friendlier to Samah. Though it would be highly unusual for Tom to allow his male son to remain in his territory, I do know that for now the relationship was at least congenial.

What was responsible for this minor miracle? Without taking any personal credit for Tom's change of heart, I do believe that the divine inner prompting to send him love and make him feel part of the family slowly altered his antisocial behavior. Although he still never allows a person to pet him, at least he does hang out with his extended family, and has stopped being an abusive father. If an attitude of love, acceptance, and inclusion can do this for a cat, imagine what it can do for human beings. It's so simple. And it doesn't require spending any money. All that's needed is for a person to value love and uncover the obstacles to giving and receiving it—be they material, technological, mental, emotional, or conditioned.

The other influence in Tom's transformation was of course Sweetie. This marvelous creature must be given the full credit she deserves. I truly believe Sweetie instinctively changed her tactic with Tom after he murdered her entire litter. Because she knew Bhakti and Samah would be safe in my room during their infancy, she really didn't spend much time with Tom except for a few hours here and there. But after the two little Lucifers were born, Sweetie spent quite a lot of time with Tom from the very beginning. So he had no reason to kill them. Yes. Instinct can be more potent than reason in both cats and humans, for better or for worse, depending on how you view it. But Tom's transformation truly reveals that even in cats, the most primal murderous instincts built in by nature can be modified by love.

Tara filled me in on some other details about the daily life of our cat family. Bhakti and Samah continue to hang out in front of my room, which is their real territory, as it was the place of their birth and growth. When it is time for lunch Tara calls, "Bhakti, Samah, lunch." And they come running down to the second floor to eat. They always eat inside at twelve. Then another minor miracle occurred. When her husband is inside with the cats, he no longer suffers from asthma. By some divine dispensation, with the help of new medicine, his cat allergy seems to have vanished! For dinner, the same scenario repeats itself. "Kittens, time to eat," yells Tara. In a flash, Bhakti and Samah come for dinner. During the day, Samah spends a lot of his time sitting high on a tree, whereas Bhakti spends most of her time hanging out in the building. The two kittens continue to enjoy the garden every afternoon.

. . .

As I sit in Central Park, where I have been sharing with you this wondrous story of the cat guru, a hose-like fountain sprays water into the pond. A rainbow appears. In a flash, I traverse the miles between India and New York. I send love to Bhakti and Samah, Sweetie and Tom, the two baby Lucifers, Tara, Lilo, Joan, Padma, Lisa, Jack, Toni and Teri, Loretta, Mr. Raj, the volunteers, the sweeper, the ashram secretary, and even the security chief—who are each a tiny spark of divine love. And so are we all.

# 32

## THE FINAL CHAPTER

Rainbows are wondrous. But as part of the world of change, even rainbows are temporary. Though I had thought that the prior chapter was the end, unforeseen events have compelled me to continue our story. Seven months later I returned to India to the ashram Prashanti Nilayam. My first stop was Tara's apartment. We greeted each other joyfully. And then. . . . "Sit down. I'll make you some herb tea."

She said nothing about the kittens till we were both seated. It wasn't difficult for me to surmise that something was gravely amiss.

She began with what I thought was the worst. "Naina, Bhakti is no more." It was a shock but something in me had suspected that might happen. "She was playing nicely here on the veranda. Then one day her two hind legs became paralyzed."

Could such a swift transition be possible? Playing nicely one minute and paralyzed the next? Maybe she never fully recuperated from her fall. But she had seemed to be improving every day.

"She stayed out here for a while and Samah brought her a pigeon. They ate together. She really enjoyed it."

"Oh, Samah really knows how to hunt without his mother teaching him." I felt grateful for small things. His nature was always so sweet and generous.

"His father took him out hunting. Remember you would tell Tom to teach the kittens how to hunt? Well, he actually listened."

What marvelous creatures these cats are!

Tara continued, "Bhakti stayed out on the veranda and would go downstairs and sit in the sand. Then her condition worsened. One day I noticed that her whole bottom was covered with red ants. So I told her, 'Bhakti, you're not going to like this, but it's for your own good.' I took her inside and dipped her in the water and washed off the ants. Then I placed her here on my bed where she stayed for a few weeks until she died."

My heart sank.

"I put a rubber sheet and some towels on the bed. When I placed plastic over the towel she would relieve herself. I sprinkled her with powder. She smelled good. She was very clean and went only on the plastic."

With great sadness I recalled the days of toilet training when they peed on newspaper and plastic bags and even in the dustpan.

"While she rested here I would give her teachings to help her soul evolve. She looked at me and really listened," Tara said.

I remembered how open and receptive these kittens were to spiritual teachings.

"At night she slept here with me. And Samah slept with my husband."

"What a sacrifice for him with his asthma," I said.

"He loved Samah," she said.

What dedicated, loving people. Had I been the caretaker, would I have put Bhakti on my bed?

"We had a little funeral ceremony for Bhakti. That helps her soul ascend to a higher birth."

"You have great compassion. You have performed a real *yajña* (sacrifice)," I said, with unfathomable gratitude.

Since Vedic times, performing actions to help animals (*bhuta yajña*) has been considered one of the five duties of human beings.[17] Each of the five kinds of dutiful action is considered a form of sacrifice.

---

17 The other four are: duty to the gods or powers of nature, to the ancestors, to the needy, and to the rishis, or teachers.

"And now for Samah," she said.

I was not at all prepared for what was to come.

"He used to go out to the garden and come back. One day he didn't return. A few days later I received a note from Lilo saying that Samah was injured. Someone left him in a box on her balcony. I went and took him to the vet. His leg was mangled and swollen. They thought it was broken. He was bitten by a dog."

I was shocked. "Samah was so quick. He could sniff a dog a mile away. I don't understand how that could happen."

"Maybe it was a whole pack of dogs and he was cornered. With no volunteers around, packs of wild dogs roamed the ashram and even came into the building. They walked up and down the stairs and ran around the veranda."

Still the story made no sense. If it were a dog, wouldn't it have killed Samah?

"Gertrude from the Animal Rescue Center took him to the vet in Bangalore. His leg was treated. Then she took him into her home where he lived with other dogs and cats."

"Is he there now?"

Tara shook her head, "My cook would stop there to inquire about Samah. His leg was healing. He would go out and come back. But the last time she went, he was gone. He never came back."

Again my heart sank, even deeper than before.

"I gave Gertrude money to feed him lamb and fish. He probably did not want dry food anymore. When he gets hungry he'll come back."

I had my doubts that Samah would ever return. With grave sadness of heart, I went to get my bags. Tomorrow the investigation would proceed.

When I finally tracked down Gertrude, she filled me in on the details. "I took Samah to the Canadian vet in Bangalore. One leg was broken, and the other was badly mangled—teeth had bitten right through. It was very swollen. The vet wanted to amputate to avoid gangrene, but I tried bandaging the legs and it worked. Samah began to heal. I kept him in our backyard in Whitefield with other kittens and cats and dogs. They all got along fine. He was very happy."

I could picture Samah romping around with the other dogs and cats. Interestingly enough, I had a dream around that time of a friendly dog licking Samah.

"Then Baba returned to Puttaparthi. Here I have no yard. The vet was afraid Samah would roam too far away and be hurt by dogs. So she told me to castrate Samah. I had him neutered. He would go out and come back, and one day he never returned."

"Maybe he's okay," I said.

"No. The villagers found his body. He was attacked by dogs."

"I don't understand," I said. "Samah was so quick. He could sense dogs minutes before they came, and he'd run away or climb up a tree. I don't understand."

Later Lilo explained it to me. "When you castrate a male cat who goes outdoors, that's his death sentence."

Male hormones are needed for fight and flight, for quickness, for survival. If for some reason it is necessary to neuter a male cat, he should not be let out unsupervised, unless he's in a yard or a sheltered environment. The streets of Puttaparthi were hardly a sheltered environment. Samah was only about seven months old at the time.

Another thing Lilo said is that sometimes a dog bites the back of a kitten and causes paralysis without any teeth marks showing. Could that have happened to Bhakti?

She suspected that Samah's legs were bitten by a male cat, as cats often bite on the legs, whereas dogs usually go for the spine or the neck. But trying to piece together the events did not really help. I cried and cried for Samah and Bhakti, and especially for Samah. I had really thought he would make it. Though the people at the Animal Rescue Center meant very well, they knew little about cats. Western methods were simply not suitable for the wildness of Puttaparthi. I hope he did not sacrifice his life in vain, and that they will learn from their mistakes. I hope they will stop neutering male cats who venture out alone in an unsheltered environment.

Alongside good intentions, knowledge is also necessary. When actions are performed in ignorance, destruction results. When partial information is mistaken for knowledge, this leads only to disaster.

I too had been ignorant of what cat survival entailed. I believed Bhakti and Samah had passed the critical period. With most of the people and cars gone from the ashram, I imagined this would be a wonderful time of transition for the kittens. As long as they had a reliable food source and a place to sleep, I thought they would thrive. I was dead wrong. If only I had given them to Jyoti to adopt. She had six cats and a couple of dogs, all playing nicely together in her fenced-in yard. But it was too late for "if only."

The next day while sitting in darshan, in heart-wrenching pain, I tried to send love to the kittens instead of wallowing in grief. This was a very difficult, ongoing struggle. But then, something unusual happened. In a flash, I saw that the souls of the kittens might have taken on an animal body for my sake. Was this their yajña, their sacrifice? Had they descended to earth so they could teach me what I needed to know, and help me complete a cycle of my karma? If so, this was a sacrifice of love. As an aspect of the Goddess, a portion of nature, they performed their task wholeheartedly, and when it was completed, the time was ripe for them to depart.

Could it be that Samah's premature death, which did not allow him to fight for territory and mate, would prevent any violent animal tendencies from forming and becoming habitual impressions in his mind? Would this not ensure a higher human birth for Samah, maybe even in a family of yogis, where nonviolence was practiced?

I am well aware that this could easily sound like a rationalization or wishful thinking. Let me assure you, this is not the case. If the thought had emerged from the mind, it would surely have been a rationalization. But the idea descended from a higher plane, from feeling-intuition. The divine informs the higher intellect through inner knowing.[18]

When you are shown that life and death are indeed in higher hands than our own or those of the medical profession, a new understanding emerges. Acceptance comes. Sadness from the human perspective

---

18 In Indian thought, the intellect (*buddhi*) functions through forethought, reasoning, evaluation, and discriminating right from wrong. The higher intellect receives intuitions directly from the divine, the total cosmic mind, when a sufficient degree of inner purification has occurred.

transforms itself into the enormous loving gratitude that I felt for these two little carriers of God energy and divine joy, who descended to earth for no other purpose than to serve and perform their dharma.

Through fully experiencing my helplessness and suffering alongside the force of love—through my feeble attempts to send love to the kittens instead of simply wallowing in grief—something painfully beautiful happened. Grace descended in the form of finer feeling, intuition, and understanding. A more inclusive level of reality was revealing herself and transforming my pain.

And what about that flash of a thought—almost forgotten—that Samah and Bhakti embodied the souls of my equal-minded father and my wholly loving grandmother? In the East, where the ancestors are revered, many people believe that the spirits of departed family members continue to help them throughout their entire lives. Never before had I considered such a possibility. Was it just a fleeting fantasy?

The great teachers of Vedanta emphasize that we are each a soul with a body, not a body with a soul. When we identify with this body-ego-mind form in time and place, we are limiting our real sense of self and are living in maya. The physical body, with all its relationships and habits is temporary. *We are each part of an ever-living continuity throughout time and space.* And when the moment of completion comes for the individual soul, it moves on. The body is simply discarded like a set of old clothes.

Lilo said that the subtle body,[19] or spirit, of pets often lingers round the home of their master. I would much prefer it if the souls of Bhakti and Samah were to ascend to higher levels, where they would remain with the Great Goddess who sent them, until their next mission of divine descent.

Before completing the final chapter, let me fill you in on a few more details. Of the two baby Lucifer Juniors, only one is left. Her name is now Baby Panther. She is shiny jet black with striking green eyes that glow in

---

19 The subtle body is considered an invisible part of each living being, and it leaves the gross body at the time of physical death. It includes the mind, intellect, ego, and memory, which is called the inner equipment or *antahkarana*. Prana is also considered part of this subtle body that is said to travel with us from life to life, until it becomes fully purified, naturally silent and still—with no more desires and nothing more to be done.

the dark. Sometimes in the black of night, all you can see are her two bright green eyes, flashing like eerie bulbs illuminating the darkness. She has the same wary personality as her father, Tom. No human being can get within a foot of her. I guess that's what's needed for an Indian cat to be a survivor—with the possible exception of Sweetie.

Tom has gotten quite thin and aged very quickly during the seven months I was away. But age has nothing to do with sex drive. Tom's still going strong! Sweetie had two more litters since the baby Lucifers, but no one has yet seen any of them, so I presume their life spans were extremely short. Still, that does not prevent Sweetie and Tom from romping.

Just yesterday, from my fourth-floor veranda, I was watching the two of them participating in their cat maya. Tom would howl—a deep yelp from the gut that could only be called a mating call. As he tried approaching Sweetie, she played a game of hard to get. She'd run around a little bit, then lie down and stretch in the sun, turn over, and wiggle back and forth, scratching her back in the sand. Tom would then try to approach her again. This time Sweetie darted away a few feet toward the tree. There she peed, all the while looking very happy and seductive. Now Tom tried again, and finally she was ready.

Sweetie began walking upstairs. After all, some things are private— even for a cat. They pranced in unison up the four flights of stairs to the roof. Here they would have the privacy and beauty to play to their hearts' content. And a new cycle of life would continue.

# EPILOGUE

Caring for animals teaches us love and compassion, and encourages us to open our hearts. But the effects are more far-reaching than simply on the personal level. Through feeding and loving animals, we can participate in maintaining the universal order and help evolution to proceed. There is a vast cosmic reason behind bhuta yajña, the Vedic sacrifice of offering food to animals.

For when a wild animal receives love from a person, its soul responds. According to esoteric teachings, an inner yearning is born to be human, like that person. The same principle operates in a human being. When a sensitive person meets a saint or a true incarnation of God, the unspoken, spontaneous inner response is, "Please God, let me be like Him. Let me be like Her. Let me be like You. Please God, let me know my true nature." In the same way that a person exposed to the higher consciousness deeply yearns to live out his or her God nature, so an inherently wild animal who is loved by human beings yearns to be human. And the ancient wisdom teaches that our next birth will be determined by our deepest desire.

This is how we all proceed upward beyond the biological evolutionary cycle into genuine spiritual evolution. A divine partnership is established to help us ascend the ladder of creation till we each embrace our God nature. We evolve both on the physical level of the body and the psychological level of the psyche—from animal to human to divine. Then when we discover our true home, which exists always, there is no more need for evolution.

The cat guru is ever teaching me faith and surrender. Faith in the wisdom of nature and the rulership of God is the catalyst for attuning one's body, mind, and intelligence to divine love and acting from that and that alone, hearing that and that alone, loving that and that alone—in everyone and everything. When the wisdom of nature is left out of the equation, it is very easy to mistake our own egoism for divine will, as the history of all religious strife reveals. Through this inclusive inner attunement, pettiness ceases, egoism dissolves, maya loosens her stubborn foothold, and we gradually become vehicles for the higher to enter into life. In this way, we can each participate in an expansive nature that includes God and in a God that includes nature.

I cannot say my last good-bye without definitely completing the saga—for now anyway. A couple of months later, Sweetie gave birth to another adorable black-and-white kitten who reminded me of Samah. Around the same time, Sweetie's daughter Baby Panther, at the fertile age of nine months, had her first litter, which consisted of three little gray-and-white stripers and one skinny jet-black kitten. It is absolutely unnecessary for me to tell you who the father was!

# POSTSCRIPT

JUST PRIOR TO PUBLICATION OF THIS BOOK, I returned to the ashram Prashanti Nilayam. Before opening the door to my room, I noticed rips, holes, and bite marks in the curtains.

My room had been invaded by mice. There was not one cat to be seen in the entire ashram. Within a week, I began hearing an isolated meow from time to time, but the source was hidden—always hidden. What happened to the cats?

After making inquiries, I was told by a longtime resident that in the 1970s the place had been inundated by rats. So someone brought in a few wild cats from the surrounding hills. Then the rats disappeared.

The cats probably had such a difficult time in the ashram because it was not their chosen territory and they were sorely outnumbered by dogs. In addition, the cat population was neither appreciated nor duly rewarded by human beings for the great service that they were performing.

But by now, we must know that this tale isn't only about cats or the delicate balance of nature or the ubiquitousness of change. Nor is our story simply about the multifaceted projections of maya. Goddess Maya continuously veils reality from us that we might come to learn how not to be ensnared in her web. For it is up to each and every one of us to perceive our story in as whole a way as possible, while participating to the best of our ability in our naturally assigned roles. And truly revel in the play!

# The Silent Oblation

And the gods descended from heaven
in the form of the animal
to perform a great sacrifice
for humankind

not through ritual slaughter
or sacred fire
there is no exalted altar here
no bloodstained knife
not even a psalm of praise

this precious sacrifice of
animal life
remains forever secret
and silent

Hear O spiritual seeker
the Lord our God
the Lord is One

the Great Goddess of no name
O omnipresent Avatar
descends to earth
to perpetuate love and
help human beings ascend
the holy mountain to liberation

in the form of bow wow
squeak or meow!

the cat goddess sacrifices
her animal body just as
the holy saint nurtures
humankind and upholds
the earth

none is too big
none is too small
no one is better or worse

we each have our own
special dharma to play
while the carousel spins and
spins round and round
this mysterious cosmos
of maya

# GLOSSARY

ANTAHKARANA: The inner equipment, the aspect of the subtle body that includes the mind, intellect, ego, and memory. This is said to travel with us from life to life until our inner purification has been completed and we come to know reality.

ASHRAM: A spiritual community or retreat. One might visit an ashram to receive spiritual teachings and strive to connect with one's inner nature.

ASURIC: The demonic nature, the major qualities of which are materialism, insensitivity, egoism, greed, hatred, anger, envy, pride, and attachment.

AVATAR: An embodiment of God in human form, who descends to earth with the express purpose of uplifting humanity, in order to nourish and maintain the world. This occurs through transforming the hearts and minds of individual men and women who make an effort to live the teachings. In India, Rama, Krishna, Buddha, and Christ are considered avatars, as are many other great teachers. One of the ten major avatars of Vishnu is a tortoise named Kurma, who held the world on his back, to prevent it from sinking into oblivion.

AYURVEDIC: An ancient Indian form of treatment that aims to balance the four elements present within the human body (air, water, fire, and earth) through herbal medicines and specific application of diet suitable for each individual. By feeling the pulse, the doctor is able to diagnose the imbalance and prescribe the appropriate medicine that will lead to harmony and healing.

BHAJANS: Devotional songs.

BHAKTI: Devotion. Bhakti is a path to realization that emphasizes love for God and seeing God in all. This is expressed through worship, devotional singing, and serving others. Bhakti is considered especially suitable for those who have an emotional, feeling temperament. No matter what one's path, devotion to the higher is essential for inner evolution.

BHUTA YAJÑA: The sacrifice of helping animals; offering them food with conscious remembrance.

BUDDHI: The intellect, which consists of the reasoning processes, discrimination (differentiating good from evil, the real from the unreal), and the higher intelligence that includes divine intuition. What we view as fact or knowledge must be evaluated by the intellect and, if possible, confirmed by the higher intellect on the path to Truth. Otherwise, knowledge remains on the level of subjectivity and opinion, if the senses and mind are the primary means of taking in perceptions and processing information. Human beings have the capacity to learn to engage these higher faculties, which can lead us to detachment, humility, and unity.

CHAKRA: A subtle center of energy or "wheel" within the body. Each individual center embodies a qualitatively different experience and meditative state, on the ladder of evolution toward the highest consciousness. Chakra can also be used to signify the totality of divine energy.

DARSHAN: Seeing; often used in the context of seeing God or seeing the guru, who is a manifestation of the divine. The darshan of Sri Sathya Sai Baba offers people the opportunity to be in the presence of an inconceivably powerful energy, which can have a far-reaching effect on their daily lives and quicken their inner evolution.

DHARMA: Duty, righteousness, or the essence of a thing. It stems from the Sanskrit root, *dhr*, to support. Therefore, righteous action is our greatest support. Our deepest dharma is to discover our true nature.

GURU: Teacher, one who imparts knowledge, both secular and spiritual. Receiving knowledge from a spiritual teacher can lead to experience and help activate the inner guru.

KALI YUGA: Our present era, the Age of Violence, is the most degenerate age, when qualities such as anger, hatred, egoism, envy, materialism, and lack of dharma predominate. The oldest era, called the *Sathya Yuga* is the most virtuous time. Human values and morality subsequently degenerate with each forthcoming age, called the *Treta Yuga* and the *Dvapara Yuga* respectively. Time in Indian thought is cyclical, and the four different eras perpetually continue throughout the millenniums until the dissolution of the world.

KARMA: Action, which is related to cause and effect. We reap what we sow. One aim of spiritual work is to purify our past thoughts, emotions and actions, and prevent new karma from forming. This occurs through conscious remembrance, and not being attached to the results of the actions we perform.

MANDIR: Temple.

MANTRA: A mantra consists of words or syllables that are repeated in an attempt to steady the wandering mind, for a calm and peaceful mind can greatly help a person to cross over the world of illusion. The technique of mantra repetition is sometimes performed with beads and should be done internally, not out loud. Traditionally, a mantra is to be given to an individual aspirant by a realized soul and is not to be connected with monetary payment. The word stems from the root *man*, which is also the same root for mind (*manas*).

MAYA: The ongoing world of change, the totality of creation, or that aspect of the Goddess within the human psyche, which causes us to believe that the limited perceptions imposed by the senses and mind are real. She veils reality from us, on the inner subjective level as well as on the outer objective level, so that through our varied experiences we can gradually evolve into a state of more expansive consciousness and leave her dominion behind. As we become more aware of her veiling power, she helps us to realize reality, including the real nature of our own soul. When we can let go of identification with our limited body-ego-mind form in time and place, then are we no longer controlled by maya. Goddess Maya is considered a projection from the mind of God, Reality, Totality. Her realm is time and space.

MULA PRAKRITI: The subtle invisible root of matter that differentiates into the material world with ongoing creation, through different stages from fine to gross, thereby becoming accessible to the senses. Matter could not exist without the presence and support of the universal spirit, the Supreme Purusha.

PRANA: The subtle universal substance of life energy present everywhere, that manifests in the body as the five vital airs: breath, circulation, digestion, elimination, and the power of thought.

PRANIC HEALING: A form of healing that works to cleanse the unhealthy energies from the aura and the subtle body.

PRASHANTI NILAYAM: The ashram of Sri Sathya Sai Baba in south India, in Andhra Pradesh. The name means "abode of peace." Scheduled activities consist of two darshans per day, as well as devotional singing and some organized lectures on Indian spirituality. During festival times, Sai Baba gives discourses.

PURANAS: A voluminous collection of stories of mythical dimension about primordial times, creation, the gods and goddesses, rishis, and great heroes of ancient India.

PURUSHA: The supreme spirit, the transcendent principle, which serves as the invisible, all-pervasive support for the immanent material world. The world could not exist without both Purusha and Prakriti, spirit and matter. The word also means "person," which implies that human beings are an embodiment of the divine.

PUTTAPARTHI: A village in South India, several hours from Bangalore, where Sri Sathya Sai Baba was born. It is the place of his ashram, Prashanti Nilayam, which has become a bustling center of pilgrimage for people throughout the world. When I first visited in 1986, the last hour of the journey was by dirt road and the main street housed one "restaurant." Now the town is bustling with high-rise apartment buildings, interesting shops, good fruit and vegetable stalls, multinational cuisine, and internet cafés—as well as scores of persistent beggars who are definitely not native! In short, peacefulness has been sacrificed for "convenience."

RISHI: A sage, seer, experiential knower of Truth. The rishis are considered the progenitors of the human race. They received divine knowledge in meditation, which they codified into the Vedas for the benefit of humanity. In India, people trace their ancestral lineage to different rishis. Some believe that the rishis continue to support the world, the human race, and help us to evolve.

SANKHYA: An ancient philosophy expounded by the rishi (sage) Kapila. The word means numbering and reveals the different stages of creation, the projection of matter from the subtlest, all pervasive, invisible level (Mula Prakriti) to the grosser levels, visible to the senses, and including the human mind and ego. Both Prakriti and Purusha are inherent in creation with Purusha as the invisible support of matter.

SEVA: Selfless service. Our work and actions become seva when they are performed with the attitude of serving the higher, and seeing the divine in the other, as well as in oneself. When we perform actions without the egocentric desire for results, our actions no longer bind our soul and our karma gradually dissolves, as there is no more fuel to feed it. Self-centered desire serves as the main fuel that continuously perpetuates our karma.

SHAMAH: Balanced under difficult circumstances; calm, equal-minded. Although this word was the inspiration for the name of the kitten Samah, I pronounced his name Samáh, which means length of time. In the south of India, the *sh* sound is often pronounced as *s*.

SHIVA: The aspect of the totality that embodies the energy of dissolution. Shiva is the God who destroys imperfection, so that life on earth can regain its basic purity and auspiciousness. When we are unable to consciously participate in dissolving our inner impurities—such as egoism, hatred, attachment, greed, rage, and envy—then destruction manifests. Since dissolution implies a new realignment of creation and the subsequent nourishing maintenance of the universe, this divine principle is viewed as encompassing the whole. It also integrates the male/female principle and implies transcendence or Absolute Consciousness. The vehicle of Shiva is the bull Nandi, symbolic of the eternal nature of dharma.

SHIVA LINGAM: A phallic or oval-shaped stone that signifies creation, regeneration, and the male and female principle. The lingam is viewed as a symbol of the formless God, which is eternal, indestructible, and present within each life form. It is used as an object of worship and healing. There are a number of lingams throughout India, which are called self-generated (*svayambhuh*), not created by any sculptor. These are considered a direct manifestation of the divine presence of Shiva.

TUSHTI: Contentment, satisfaction, calmness. Nine different kinds of contentment are delineated in Sankhya philosophy.

VISHNU: The aspect of the totality that embodies the energy of preservation. Vishnu is the god who protects, sustains, and nourishes humanity and helps life on earth to continue. The avatars are considered to be divine incarnations of Vishnu, as they all descend to earth to help preserve humanity, when life becomes chaotic due to lack of goodness and dharma.

VRITTI: Movement, mode of action, fluctuations of the mind. An aim of yoga is to calm the movements of the mind and body, thereby ending restlessness and distraction, making room for a more expansive inner experience.

YAJÑA: Sacrifice. According to Vedanta philosophy, the entire creation is continuously involved in some form of cosmic sacrifice. Therefore, through our human birth, we are being offered the opportunity to participate either consciously or unconsciously—with an inner striving that helps the cosmos, or with the automatic inevitability that temporarily hinders our personal and universal evolution. In India, people apply this principle of yajña in a practical way through five forms of sacrifice, which offer a daily framework for participating in the evolution of the universe. These five yajñas are: our duty to animals, *bhata yajña*; to the gods or nature, *deva yajña*; to the ancestors, *pitr yajña*; to the needy, *nri yajña*; and lastly, duty to the teachers, which consists of offering one's individual soul to the all-pervading universal essence, *Brahma yajña*. Living consciously in this way helps the universe, as well as our individual soul.

# ABOUT THE AUTHOR

NAINA LEPES BEGAN A LONG TERM relationship with cats when a beautiful black-and-white stray crawled through a tiny opening in her sixth floor kitchen window and remained for fourteen years. But this experience did not adequately prepare her for the whirlwind of being a foster mother to a semiwild cat family in India.

Naina is a longtime student of Vedanta and Eastern spirituality, whose teachers include Sri Sathya Sai Baba, Swami Chinmayananda, and Sri Karunamayi. She is the author of *The Bhagavad Gita and Inner Transformation* and a Web site on the *Gita* at *www.thegitaspace.com*. Formerly, she worked as a Jungian psychotherapist and has also participated in the work of G. I. Gurdjieff. Her formal education includes degrees in music, psychology, and counseling. Naina lives in India and New York.